WALKING WITH CONTEMPLATION

A Walker's Guide

Edited by
P.K. Colleran

Cafh Foundation, Inc.
Berkeley, California
1983

Library of Congress Catalog Card Number: 82-72569

International Standard Book Number: 0-9609102-0-4

Cafh Foundation, Inc.
P.O. Box 4665
Berkeley, California 94704

Typesetting by Gregory L. Vierra
Word Processing Center
University of California
Berkeley

Printed in the United States of America

To the ginkgo tree

CONTENTS

Prologue

For the last five years, Sunday mornings have brought a new type of visitor to the parks of the San Francisco Bay Area. Like most visitors to these beautiful bay hills, this group is made up of walkers. But there is something different about these organized hikes through the hills. They have an added dimension to them: a method of life, a means of discovering meaning through contemplation.

Walking with Contemplation is the name of this series of walks sponsored by Cafh Foundation, Inc., a nonprofit educational and spiritual organization. The walks are open to the public in general, and the people who have participated are from varied occupations and backgrounds. They are manual workers, students, teachers, retired workers, younger and older persons, men and women, singles and couples. Meeting a few Sunday mornings each month, they come together to walk in silence through the redwood-tree trails, some sightseeing and others simply in a state of recollection. After a short hike, the group sits in a circle to listen to a prepared presentation about the life and work of a great person whose existence has relevance and meaning. The time after the talk is spent sharing ideas raised by the biography, walking back through the woods, and enjoying refreshments and good conversation.

This activity was inspired by the proposition that the integral education of any human being shall include the study of these three fields: philosophy of history, natural sciences, and biographies of great beings. The series, Walking with Contemplation, has been a practical way of exploring this last field by investigating the teachings and lives of many great contemporary persons. Combined with walking, it has become a new way to study, enjoy physical exercise, and meet new companions. Walking has always been a means of reflecting and exploring meaning in life. Aristotle taught his disciples while walking and by doing so formed the Peripatetic School. The journey of the Russian Pilgrim was his way of learning unceasing prayer. And Gandhi--one of the great contemporary lives studied in this series--used walking as a means of meditation.

And so this book was born. Out of the shared experience, enjoyment, and fruits of these walks came the inspiration for a book--a book to be used by walkers. The first part of this book is a series of biographies, written with the hope that walkers will read them and find inspiration to apply to their own lives. The second part is about the art of walking, covering practical topics ranging from the importance of walking for physical and mental exercise, what are the necessary implements to bring walking, to how to organize walks. Many different groups of people will find useful information in this book. This book is designed to be used by walkers while walking, to be brought along as a welcome companion for inspirational ideas as well as practical advice. It can also be used by families or groups of individuals who would like to organize a series of Walking with Contemplation like those sponsored by Cafh Foundation. Finally, this book will be a handy tool for educators and leaders of scouting groups, environmentalists' associations, summer camps, and many other recreational institutions.

Special thanks are extended to Sandra Rowland, Joan Ehara, and Carlos Benito for editorial advice and numerous helpful suggestions; to Valeria Evans for her kind patience in listening to me throughout the many months of preparation of this book; and, of course, to the authors of each biography, without whom this book would not exist.

P. K. Colleran
Berkeley, California
May, 1982

INTRODUCTION

The series, Walking with Contemplation, is more than five years old by now--more than sufficient time for a tree to bear fruit. Learning about great beings, exercising through walking, contemplating nature, and being convivial were a few of the fruits harvested by us. In addition, researching, communicating, and serving were the fruits of the persons in charge of each program. But Walking with Contemplation, like all of life's experiences, has given to us a more essential fruit, a teaching.

The practice of Walking with Contemplation resembles the life of a human being, for we can look at life as a road to be traversed. This road, the entire existence of a person, is made of many trails and paths. If we were able to look at the road from above we could discern where it points to. But the wayfarer--each one of us--lives and walks down in the valleys and deep forests of human life. One does not know where these trails lead to, how many of them exist, what wonders and perils surround them. One may not even know what to walk for. Each person is confronted with the task of discovering the meaning of his life, and then of learning to live and fulfill his possibilities. Experience indicates that the way of learning about a road is to traverse its trails; it is to begin walking and, then, at the end of the journey to find out if the place one arrives to is the one that was yearned for.

This does not mean that one has to traverse life under complete ignorance and uncertainty. One can always find some guidance and help, and one can always learn from his experiences. Indeed, when the pioneers walked toward new, unknown frontiers, they were preceded by brave and skillful scouts--those who had ventured before in a solitary way. Similarly, when a group of friends walk in darkness, they follow one who previously blazed the trail.

The life of each human being that we chose to learn and to meditate about during one of our walks represents for us a light blazing a stage of our road. His or her life helps us to realize what is the purpose of human existence and how to live our lives accordingly. The different situations and places in which these persons found themselves varied enormously, from Mahatma Gandhi in South Africa and India under the British rule, Thomas Merton in a Trappist monastery, Albert Schweitzer in Africa, Simone Weil in France before and during the Nazi occupation, to W. B. Yeats in an Ireland struggling for its political independence. Different also were their specific tasks: Dorothy Day working for the poor in New York, Mother Teresa caring for those dying in the streets of Calcutta, Carl Jung investigating the depths of the human soul, Maria Montessori working for a more expansive education for children, and so on. From all this diversity we have learned, but we have learned even more from their common traits: their decision to live with a transcendent view of existence, their willingness to transform themselves in order to fulfill their missions, and their fidelity to their vocation until the last breath of their existence.

These beings are called great or inspiring because they have opened and blazed new trails for humanity. But this is also the case with each human being. At each moment of daily life, one leaves an open trail--a road already traversed. At the same time, one is confronted with new roads. Our responsibility is to choose one of them and to fulfill it.

Each walk and talk is helping us to broaden the meaning of our individual journeys, our lives. We are becoming more aware that Walking with Contemplation is more than a symbol. It is the living image of human life.

Part One

BIOGRAPHIES OF GREAT BEINGS

ALBERT SCHWEITZER
Reverence for Life

Much talk is heard in our times about building a new human race. How are we to build a new humanity? Only by leading men toward a true, inalienable ethic of our own . . . Reverence for Life . . . Reverence for Life comprises the whole ethic of love in its deepest and highest sense. It is the source of constant renewal for the individual and for mankind.

Albert Schweitzer was a great being whose life of offering and service to humanity has had a profound effect on the world. Throughout his lifetime, he developed his extraordinary intellectual and artistic gifts, making important contributions in philosophy, Christian theology, and music. But, at the same time, he was always sensitive to the suffering in the world and came to realize that his vocation was to renounce his gratifying scholarly and creative pursuits in order to more directly serve humanity.

Albert Schweitzer was born in 1875 in Alsace, a historically disputed region between France and Germany. He was the son of a minister and the grandson of an organist. He showed musical talent at an early age and soon became the substitute organist

11

at his father's church. He enjoyed his father's services very much and yearned to become a minister himself. As a boy, Albert was exposed to a unique form of cooperation where Catholics and Protestants shared the same church buildings. This instilled in him an openness and respect for all people and an understanding that all religions and philosophies share a common essence.

At the age of ten, he moved in with his godparents and entered the Gymnasium. At first he was a poor student, but he soon learned self-discipline and proper study habits and developed more confidence. He had difficulties in mathematics and languages but gave special effort to the subjects in which he had no apparent talent. His favorite subjects were the natural sciences, history, Latin, Greek, and music--especially the organ. While at the Gymnasium, Dr. Wehman, one of Albert's professors, became his model for the fulfillment of duty. Each lesson that the teacher gave was carefully and completely prepared. Schweitzer was to carry on this example of perfection in all of his own work.

After graduation from the Gymnasium, his uncle arranged music lessons for Albert in Paris by the famous organist, Charles-Marie Widor. Schweitzer excelled under his teacher and the two cultivated a deep and long-lasting friendship.

At the age of 18, Schweitzer became a student at Strasbourg University where he studied philosophy, theology, and music. During the next 12 years, Schweitzer lived as student, teacher, minister, and musician in Strasbourg, Paris, and Berlin. He earned doctorates in his three areas of study; the first he finished at the age of 24, writing about the religious philosophy of Kant. The second, completed when he was 26, was a study of the Synoptic Gospels. And at 30, he finished his third, writing about the music of Bach.

Along with studying and playing Bach's music, Schweitzer became an expert on organ building and restoration. One of his lifelong pursuits was to encourage the restoration of the fine old church organs instead of their replacement with new organs of lower quality.

Schweitzer was quite extraordinary in the variety and depth of his knowledge and in the intensity and devotion that he had for learning. The ideas that he shared from his many fields of study were unique and of the highest quality. But in spite of his propensity for the academic and artistic life, he was called to renounce all this in order to offer his life more directly in helping to alleviate the suffering in the world.

It is clear that Schweitzer was sensitive to suffering at an early age. Several events occurred in his youth which, because of his disposition for inner reflection, his wise understanding of his own nature, and his dedication to carrying out decisions, became points of self-transformation. For example, he once saw an old horse struggling to pull a very heavy cart while being beaten mercilessly by its owners. The pain that he felt in seeing such cruelty made him realize how insensitive we are to other life forms. From then on he prayed for the protection of "everything that breathes." Later, in the development of his ethic of "Reverence for Life," he understood that any ethical philosophy must include respect and love for all life.

Young Albert's awareness of his inability to resist the impulse to assert power over his pet dog caused him to suffer and later prevented him from enjoying trained animal acts in the circus because of the necessary suffering the training entailed.

Once, when he and a friend were hunting and preparing to shoot at a flock of birds, Albert responded to a sudden urge and frightened the birds away so that they would be spared any suffering. This incident was important because not only did he awaken to the understanding that hunting and fishing for sport were cruel and unnecessary, but he also realized the need to be free of the fear of others, to not be afraid of being laughed at by friends. He worked to overcome his desire to please others and to follow their options. Instead, he transcended his shyness and became rather argumentative, searching passionately for truth by thinking things through clearly and logically. His independent approach to truth led him into conflicts. He had difficulties in his confirmation class because he was troubled by the literal truth of the Bible. Having his own spiritual ideas, he was unable to accept many of the dogmatic interpretations that he was taught.

Schweitzer's calling was to eventually leave the realm of discussion and persuasion and to make his life his argument. His work for humanity was to become the fullest expression of his inner yearnings.

This calling came to him one beautiful spring morning as he awoke. He was 21 years old and at home with his family on vacation from the university. Reflecting on his life, he realized how ideal it was. Living in an atmosphere of love and material comfort, he had wonderful opportunities to develop himself in every way. His life was one of peace and happiness. But, as a boy, he had always been bothered by the fact that his life had been blessed by such goodness while many others suffered. It upset him to know that he had better food at home than his classmates did. On one occasion, he had even refused to wear a new coat that had been given to him because his friends could not afford such a fine one. By not wanting to appear privileged in front of his friends, he participated in their poverty in a quiet and humble way.

Schweitzer knew that he could not accept his happiness as a matter of course. He owned something in return.

He decided that fine spring morning to continue on in his academic and musical interests until he reached the age of 30, at which time he would dedicate his life to some form of direct service to humanity. He later explained that "whoever is spared personal pain must feel himself called to help in diminishing the pain of others."

Schweitzer began his search for the way in which he could best serve humanity by becoming involved with various organizations and social projects, including work with abandoned and neglected children, tramps and discharged prisoners, and poor families living in slums. After each of these efforts, the feeling persisted that he needed to find a way to do his work of service in a more direct, personal, and independent way, outside of organizations. He benefited from working with these groups, however, in that he was forced to appeal for donations by going door to door. At first, he had great difficulties in doing this because of his shyness. But, he persevered and eventually overcame his fears. This experience later proved valuable when he sought support for his own humanitarian projects.

Just before his thirtieth birthday, Schweitzer read in a magazine published by the Paris Missionary Society an appeal for doctors to serve in a Congo mission. This immediately attracted him, and he soon decided to study for the degree of Doctor of Medicine so as to offer services to the Africans. He felt Africa was a particularly significant place to work because of the need to make atonement for the European colonialism and the exploitation of Africa and its people.

After completing several years of strenuous and difficult studies, Schweitzer offered himself as a medical doctor to the Paris Missionary Society. But because his previous writings, especially his study of Jesus from a psychological and historical perspective, were perceived by the Society as unorthodox and heretical, his offer was rejected. He persisted, though, by convincing the members that he was offering himself only as a physician and by pledging not to preach heresy. He also agreed to be financially responsible for the maintenance of his own mission. This he was to do for many years by using the proceeds from organ recitals which he gave throughout Europe.

Many of his friends and relatives felt that he was foolish to give up his many fine professions as professor, minister, writer, and musician. They argued that he could actually do more for the Africans by staying in Europe, speaking about their plight and soliciting donations for their aid. But his decision to go to the African jungle was based on much deeper reasons.

Schweitzer actually had serious doubts about Christian theology, especially its historical inconsistencies. He also felt that Christianity had become too complicated and abstract. Because of these doubts, he felt that he could no longer continue in his role of minister and theologian. Instead, he needed to live the spiritual ideas about which he had been teaching and writing, to translate them into a life of renouncement. He yearned to express his life in a simple way that was consistent with what he believed to be the essential teaching of Jesus: to love.

As he was completing his studies and making plans for the African venture, Albert married Helene Bresslau, the daughter of one of his professors. She went with him to found the hospital at Lambarene and worked with him as a nurse. Ill health, however, prevented Helene from staying in Africa to be with Albert. In spite of long periods of separation, she remained his beloved and faithful companion throughout the African work. She accompanied him by raising their daughter, Rhena, in Europe and by traveling and speaking throughout Europe and America to raise funds and gather volunteers for the hospital.

Schweitzer dedicated the rest of his life to working as a doctor in Africa. Except for a period during and after the First World War, the hospital at Lambarene operated continuously. It was relocated once and eventually developed into a village with several buildings, some containing medical wards, including ones for patients suffering from leprosy and mental illness. Other buildings were devoted to housing the hospital staff and families and friends of the patients. The healthy members of this community were expected to work for the benefit for those who were sick.

Schweitzer designed the hospital to reflect the cultural habits of the Africans and to provide medical services in a comfortable and familiar environment. A sterile modern hospital would not have been appropriate. He became an expert in architecture, designing buildings that could withstand the harsh weather of the tropics and made important research contributions in tropical medicine.

In spite of his decision to devote his life to the work in Africa, Schweitzer maintained strong ties to Europe and the rest of the world. He left Africa periodically to visit his wife and daughter and to give speeches and organ recitals. He carried on an enormous correspondence with his friends and admirers from around the world, attempting to write personally whenever possible. Also, he continued to write prolifically on many subjects, including comparisons in the thinking and philosophies of Eastern and Western cultures, often expressing his grave concern for humanity's destiny.

As his work in Africa progressed, Schweitzer painfully observed the disintegration of Western culture in Europe. It was difficult for him to explain to the Africans, whose culture valued community stability and personal worth, the reasons for so much bloodshed and destruction in such an advanced civilization as Europe. He felt that spiritual decadence was caused by the lack of clear, rational thinking and by the destruction of the individual in the ever-increasing mass society. Western culture was no longer truly life affirming.

Schweitzer's response came in his ethic of Reverence for Life. In his book by this title, he writes that this philosophy is based on observation that the universe is amoral, neutral.

"All thinking must renounce the attempt
to explain the universe. What is glorious
in it is united with what is full of horror.
What is full of meaning is united with
what is senseless. The spirit of the universe is at once creative and destruc-
tive--it creates what it destroys and destroys what it creates, and therefore it
remains to us a riddle. And we must
inevitably resign ourselves to this."

What is significant about Schweitzer's philosophy
is that it is man's purpose to give life meaning, to
bring ethics into existence. By recognizing and
understanding the universal will to live and by having
an attitude of reverence for all life, humanity will
have transcendent meaning to live by.

Reverence for Life is not an absolute ethic
because one recognizes that some life must be sacri-
ficed in order to preserve other life, "but never
without the realization that there is a great chain of
life from which we are not separate, and that in the
death of any life, we too suffer a loss." This attitude
towards the world eliminates the separativity between ourselves and others and emphasizes the inter-
dependency that we all share. We realize our part in
humanity and how our lives are integrated into the
lives of those around us and beyond.

Schweitzer understood that ethics must ultimately be practiced on a personal level. An ethical
person must ask himself how much of his life, his
possessions, his rights, his happiness, his time and his
rest may he keep for himself and how much must he
devote to others. Schweitzer recognized that his life
was not his own to do with as he pleased. He felt

obliged to offer his life in service to humanity, taking for himself only that which was absolutely necessary and nothing more.

On the material level, Schweitzer was aware of the illusion of private property. Since we really own nothing, we have the responsibility of stewards or trustees, not of possessors or owners. Our freedom lies in how we administer these trusts.

And on the social level, he believed that we do not actually possess social rights in the context of ethical living. We see ourselves as debtors repaying what we owe to humanity. The happier I am, the better my life has been, the more I owe in return. Also, I do not have the right to compete against my fellows if I succeed or advance at the cost of others. There should always be an inward concern for all human destinies.

Humility is an important aspect of Schweitzer's ethics. As an example of our lack of humility, he spoke of how we often use forgiveness for self-gratification. Ordinarily, when we forgive someone, we imply a subtle humiliation of him while expecting to be commended for our self-devotion. But an attitude of humility does not allow us to forgive in that fashion because we are aware of our own imperfections--the falsehoods, hatred, and arrogance--hidden in our hearts. Pardoning others is really an illusion, according to Schweitzer, because we cannot set ourselves apart from others to pass such a judgment. He saw the struggle against evil in the world to a great extent as a struggle within our own being. Instead of judging others, we need to judge and transform ourselves.

Schweitzer's life was a life of renouncement. When he gave up his successful and satisfying life in

Europe to work as a jungle doctor, he demonstrated the importance of transcending the desire for personal benefits and rewards.

Ironically, Schweitzer's renouncement was more difficult and painful for his family and friends than it was for him. He knew that he had a calling to serve humanity and felt very fortunate to have found such an ideal opportunity to express in a direct and concrete way his love for the world and his compassion for those who suffer. He was deeply thankful for his vigor and health and for the kindness and care that had been given to him. He returned these blessings through a humble offering of his life.

His humble work as a doctor in the African jungle symbolizes our need to participate, to expand our love, to renounce personal benefits, and to transform and offer our lives to humanity. His deep respect for all living creatures represents the need to respond to our highest aspirations and to recognize the world and our existence as expressions of the Divine.

Albert Schweitzer's life was an expression of divine love in the world. His inner devotion was expressed in a life dedicated to serving humanity and the world. He touched those near him by his kindness and his respect for everyone and everything. He touched the rest of the world as an eternal symbol, representing our deepest yearnings and highest aspirations.

Based on the presentation by Gregory Bennett.
Opening quotation from Albert Schweitzer, <u>Reverence for Life</u>.

References and Recommended Readings

Schweitzer, Albert. <u>On the Edge of the Primeval Forest</u>. New York: The Macmillan Company, 1936.

_____. <u>Out of My Life and Thought</u>. New York: H. Holt and Company, 1949.

_____. <u>The Philosophy of Civilization</u>. New York: The Macmillan Company, 1949.

_____. <u>Pilgrimage to Humanity</u>. New York: Philosophical Library, 1961.

_____. <u>Reverence for Life</u>. New York: Harper and Row, 1969.

ANNE SULLIVAN MACY
Teacher

*Religion is a way of living and not of
believing only. Bear witness to what
appears true to you in deeds rather than
words. Through the ages people have torn
each other to pieces over religious
beliefs, and what good has that done? Far
better it is to help others to live and live
well. Try not to grieve any heart or
disturb any soul in its effort to think
intelligently and act nobly.*

By the time she was ten years old in 1876, Anne
Sullivan Macy had met more adversity than most
people see in a lifetime. She had lost her mother,
been deserted by her father, put in a home for the
poor with her lame brother (who died there of
tuberculosis) and left nearly blind by a childhood
disease. Yet this woman, from whom fate had taken
so much, retained a tremendous capacity to give. To
Helen Keller--blind and deaf from early
childhood--she gave the ability to communicate, the
gift of language, of joyful appreciation for life's
beauty, and, most precious of all, the gift of lifelong
friendship.

Annie Sullivan arrived at the Keller home in
Alabama in the early spring of 1887. She was but 21

23

years old, with only six years of schooling herself. Helen was six, strong, stubborn, and spoiled--in her own words, ". . . a Phantom living in a world that was no world." Annie Sullivan proved to be every bit as spirited and determined as her young pupil. Not with elegant theories, but with love, unfailing inventiveness and perseverance, she rescued Helen from a world of darkness, solitude, and chaos.

From the beginning, Annie Sullivan sensed that Helen would "succeed beyond her wildest dreams." Helen described her beloved teacher as "a conceiver, a trail breaker, a pilgrim of life's wholeness." Annie devoted her life to helping Helen overcome the limitations which her handicaps imposed upon her. Together they embarked upon a lifelong journey of discovery, constantly pushing back the boundaries of Helen's capacity to directly experience, communicate, and participate in the world around her.

Annie and Helen journeyed far from the sleepy Alabama town where the first "miracles" were worked: to Boston to further Helen's education, across the continent and eventually around the world. They knew the leading social and political figures of their time: Mark Twain, Alexander Graham Bell, Dr. Edward Everett Hale, Andrew Carnegie. Active in various progressive movements, they waged a universal struggle against limitations, especially those created and perpetuated by man: poverty, war, and prejudice.

In her book, Teacher, Helen Keller refers to "the shaping fire of Teacher's spirit." Annie Sullivan sent a spark into the dark and solitary world of a blind and deaf child, kindled a flame in her heart, and devoted her life to feeding and tending that flame. From her life there is much we can learn about the power of love, imagination, and perseverance, and of the miracles that can be wrought when all of one's energies are focused on a single goal of perfection.

A daughter of Irish immigrants, Annie Sullivan was born into squalid poverty in Feeding Hills, Massachusetts, on April 4, 1866. Her mother died when Annie was eight, leaving two other children. Her father abandoned all three a few years later, and Annie never learned what became of him. Her younger sister was placed with relatives. Annie and her seven-year-old brother were sent to the State Almshouse at Tewksbury--Annie, because she was difficult to manage and too blind to be useful; Jimmie, because he was becoming hopelessly lame with a tubercular hip.

They entered the almshouse in February of 1876, and Jimmie died in May. Annie was totally desolate at the loss of the only source and object of her love. No one outside was interested in her, and she had no friends but her fellow paupers. Death and deformity were commonplace. Annie stayed there for four years. A priest befriended her and arranged for her to have an operation on her eyes. This operation was not successful, but Annie had traveled beyond the walls of the poorhouse and now she longed for escape. She learned from a fellow inmate that there were special schools for the blind.

Her opportunity came when a group of investigators commissioned by the State Board of Charities arrived at Tewksbury. Annie had learned the name of the chairman of the group, and when the committee members arrived, she flung herself toward them, unable to distinguish one from another, and cried out, "Mr. Sanborn, Mr. Sanborn, I want to go to school."

25

She was sent to the Perkins Institution, a school for the blind in Boston, in October of 1880. Outside the walls of Tewksbury, she felt the shame of poverty for the first time. Shabbily dressed, she was 14 and could neither read nor write. The other girls made fun of her. She was bewildered and rebellious.

Annie chafed against the discipline of her teachers and resisted all of their attempts to help her to learn things in which she was not interested. It took the sewing teacher two years to persuade her to finish an apron which could have been made in a couple of hours. "Sewing and crocheting," she said when she was teaching those skills to Helen, "are inventions of the devil, I think. I'd rather break stones on the king's highway than hem a hankerchief."

There was one teacher whose gentleness tamed her, and she introduced Annie to the beauty of language. In this class, she read the plays of Shakespeare. And she discovered poetry, which she found to be a noble and spiritualizing influence.

While she was at Perkins, Annie learned the manual alphabet so that she might be able to talk to Laura Bridgman, then 50, the most famous of Perkin's graduates. Laura Bridgman had been left at the age of two without sight, hearing, smell or taste, from an attack of scarlet fever. Dr. Samuel Gridley Howe, a philanthropist and progressive thinker of his time, had taught Laura language by means of raised type letters and the manual alphabet. The systematic scientific records of his pioneering work with Laura later proved an invaluable resource for Annie Sullivan's work with Helen Keller.

The school had facilities for taking care of its pupils during vacations, and one summer Annie was sent to a rooming house in Boston to do light work.

Through one of the lodgers, she found her way to the Massachusetts Eye and Ear Infirmary. Over the next 12 months, two operations and various treatments restored a good deal of her vision. She was able to read books in the ordinary way for limited periods of time, but not well enough to warrant transfer to a school for the seeing. Annie remained at Perkins for six years, graduating in 1886, valedictorian of her class.

Meanwhile, the Keller family had learned of Dr. Howe's work with Laura Bridgman and had written to the Perkins Institution at the suggestion of Alexander Graham Bell. Mr. Anagnos, then director of Perkins, recommended Annie for the position. Annie had been living on Cape Cod with Mrs. Hopkins, a matron from the school whom she had befriended. She returned to Boston to carefully study Dr. Howe's reports, a painful task because of the condition of her eyes. She accepted the position, not out of any inspired call to duty, but because circumstances made it necessary for her to earn a living, and this was the first opportunity which presented itself. Half-blind, possessed with a meager education, there was little reason to suspect she had any special fitness for the work.

Yet, on March 3, 1887, she arrived in Tuscumbia, Alabama, exhausted and homesick, her eyes reddened from the long train ride. On first meeting Helen, Annie's thoughts were that the child was like a young colt, quick-tempered, willful, and intelligent. Annie's great concern was learning how to discipline Helen without breaking her spirit.

Initially, she planned to go slowly, to gradually win the love and trust of her young charge. But, Helen would have none of it. They battled daily to stalemate, for as soon as Annie would attempt to discipline Helen, her family would intervene. She finally persuaded the Kellers of the necessity of removing Helen from her family. The two of them went to live in a little garden house not far from the main house. Here, totally dependent of her teacher, Helen took the first step in her education: she learned obedience. She learned to channel her abundant energies, to work quietly, with concentration, on manual tasks.

From the first, Annie had spelled constantly into Helen's hand, not letters, but words. Helen was very bright and learned quickly, but still had no idea that everything had a name. On April 5, little more than a month after Annie had come to Alabama, the next big breakthrough occurred. Helen was holding a mug under the spout while Annie pumped water. As cold water gushed forth, filling the mug, Annie spelled W-A-T-E-R into Helen's free hand. The word, coming together with the sensation of cold water rushing over her hand, seemed to startle Helen. She dropped the mug and stood as one transfixed. A new light came into her face. At last, she understood the meaning of words. She felt joy for the first time since her illness, and began running from object to object, begging for each word. Affection was born between teacher and pupil.

Helen turned to Annie and asked for her name. She spelled: T-E-A-C-H-E-R.

That day held a special joy for Annie. When Annie finally got into bed that night, Helen stole into her arms of her own accord and kissed her for the first time. "I thought my heart would burst, it was so full of joy," she said. Helen's love helped to dispel the loneliness that had tracked Annie since her brother's death.

Annie had observed Helen's 15-month-old cousin and deduced that the way in which normal children learned language was by imitation and repetition. She resolved to treat Helen just like a two-year-old, to talk into her hand just as she would talk into a baby's ear. All day long, as they played, as they took their long walks, as they went to visit with relatives, Annie kept spelling into her pupil's hand. She used whole sentences, repeating them many times during a day. At first, Helen absorbed much more than she could understand, but she was in constant contact with a living language. Annie felt strongly that language had a purpose: the communication of thought. Thus, Helen learned new words and phrases at the same time that she was building up a store of experiences about which to talk. Annie became her pupil's eyes and ears.

Annie's work with Helen took her into uncharted territory--there was no textbook to consult, no colleague with whom to confer. She learned to trust her own ability to discern Helen's needs and to respond to them.

Helen's daily lessons were drawn from life, shaped and inspired by her natural curiosity. Annie's energy and imagination rose to the constant challenge of Helen's seemingly insatiable appetite for knowledge. Annie missed no opportunity to teach Helen something. Wherever she went, she took Helen, and whatever she saw, she would explain to the child. Helen learned to distinguish flowers by their forms and odors. Annie caught squealing pigs and held them while Helen ran her hands over them. When the circus came to town, Helen shook hands with a bear, hugged a lion cub, rode an elephant, and was lifted up so she could feel the ears of a giraffe.

29

In some ways, they were like children growing up together. Helen's questions kept Annie busy, reading to find answers and pondering how to convey the information. She vowed to answer all of Helen's questions to the best of her ability and in a way that would be intelligible and truthful to Helen.

The reading taxed her eyes severely. This aspect of her work involved a constant sacrifice. Her eyes had never fully recovered from the operations and reading put a constant strain on them. But, she searched constantly for treasures of knowledge to share with Helen.

Helen's questions often prodded her to examine her own values. When Helen began to ask where new puppies and calves and babies came from, Annie had no one to whom she could turn for advice. She reasoned that if it was natural for Helen to ask, then it was her responsibility to answer her: "It is a great mistake, I think, to put children off with falsehoods and nonsense, when their growing powers of observation and discrimination excite in them a desire to know about things." Annie took Helen up in a tree for a long talk about plant and animal life, about seeds and eggs. She passed lighly over the function of sex, but conveyed the idea that love was the great continuer of life.

Soon, Annie reached the limits of her own knowledge and resources to teach Helen, and so the two of them set out for Boston. Helen studied at the Perkins Institution, still under Annie's personal tutelage, but with access to the extensive Braille library. They also went to New York so that Helen might study at the Wright-Humason School for the Deaf, known for its instruction in oral language. Helen finally learned to speak, but her inflection and tone were such that few could understand her well. With her teacher's support and companionship, Helen did quite well at both schools. Some time during this period, Helen got it into her mind that she would go to Radcliffe to try her lot among the seeing and hearing.

For the next few years, they prepared for the entrance examinations, first at a private girl's school in Cambridge and then under private tutors. Annie was at Helen's side, constantly interpreting to her the instructions of classroom teachers, reading and translating what could not be attained in Braille, responding to Helen's endless stream of questions. Helen passed the exams and was admitted to Redcliffe. She not only finished her courses in four years, but graduated with honors. A herculean task for both women, but as always, Annie was inspired by her vision of "perfection"--of helping Helen to be all that she could be.

Annie resisted all effort to canonize Helen or to mystify her own efforts. She never minimized the devastating effect of the deafness and blindness but neither did she relax her standards of excellence for Helen. It was her characteristic to be both scrupulously honest and straightforward. Addressing a group of teachers for the deaf, she tried to convince them that Helen was neither a "phenomenal child, an intellectual prodigy, nor an extraordinary genius, but simply a very bright and lovely child unmarred by self-consciousness or any taint of evil. Every thought mirrored on her beautiful face, beaming with intelligence and affection, is a fresh joy . . . she impresses me every day as being the happiest child in the world, and so it is a special privilege to be with her." Between them was an ever-grateful exchange.

Over the course of their years together, their relationship underwent a subtle transformation. Although Helen continued to be physically dependent on Annie, their friendship deepened so that in other ways they were equals. Helen still looked to Annie for advice and stimulation, but developed her own ideas about politics and religion. It is a mark of Annie's integrity and devotion that she encouraged Helen to develop this independence of mind and spirit.

Helen became a follower of Swedenborg and found solace in her faith. Annie did not believe, as Helen did, in a given religious creed or in immortality. She believed that religion was a way of living and not of believing only, and that tolerance was necessary between human beings.

Both women were socialists and pacifists and active in the progressive movements of the early part of the 20th century. Short of funds, Helen and her teacher accepted an offer to tour with a vaudeville show and speak to audiences. Although Helen was always greeted with waves of affection, the touring was grueling. Many people were also disturbed by Helen's public opinions about the war or labor struggles, thinking it better for their "little saint" to restrict herself to working for the handicapped. In fact, although they continued to struggle against all limitations imposed by man's ignorance, in time their efforts were focused on behalf of the blind. They traveled and lectured widely, raising funds for the American Foundation for the Blind.

As Annie's health and sight began to fail, Dolly Thomson came to live with them in 1914. She stayed for the remaining 22 years of Annie's life and continued to accompany Helen. In her final years,

Annie's eyes failed her completely. She could never quite adjust to the darkness or the dependency, but when she died on October 20, 1936, it was with few regrets, her life's work done.

Anne Sullivan Macy was neither a saint nor a "school-marm." Her life was a movement toward perfection--a struggle to overcome limitations, her own and those of her famous pupil. She had many obstacles to overcome: the emotional and material poverty of her childhood, her meager education, her impaired vision, and the undertow of her powerful temperment. But, she overcame these obstacles and transformed her own stubborn willfulness into a patient and enduring resolve.

She came to her life's work with little training or preparation, but in the end this proved a blessing of sorts. Free of preconceived notions, she was able to discover a method of teaching which was truly inno-vative. She was never afraid to experiment, to learn through observation and trial, guided always by the spontaneous impulses of her pupil. We teach what we are, not with intellectual convictions or theories. Annie Sullivan bestowed her youth, her vitality, her extraordinary zest for living, her love of beauty and language on Helen.

Anne Sullivan Macy not only freed a soul locked in a prison of darkness and silence, but nurtured and guided her through a friendship that spanned nearly 50 years. Another famous teacher, Maria Montessori, expressed it this way in a tribute to teacher and pupil:

> "Helen Keller is a marvelous example of the phenomenon common to all human beings--the possibility of the liberation of

the imprisoned spirit of man by the
education of the senses. Here lies the
basis of the method of education."

Based on the presentation by Laura Peck.
Opening quotation from Teacher, by Helen Keller.

References and Recommended Readings

Braddy, Nellie (Henny). Anne Sullivan Macy. New
York:Doubleday, 1933.

Keller, Helen. Teacher: Anne Sullivan Macy. New
York:Doubleday, 1955.

_____. The Story of My Life. New York: Andor,
1976.

Lasche, Joseph P. Helen and Teacher: The Story of
Anne Sullivan Macy and Helen Keller. New
York:Delacourte Press/Seymour Lawrence, 1980.

THOMAS MERTON
Monk and Modern Mystic

> *Our real journey in life is interior; it is a matter of . . . deepening, and of an ever greater surrender to the creative action of love and grace in our hearts. Never was it more necessary for us to respond to that action.*

Many moderns believed religion to be a relic of the past, unnecessary in an age of industrial enlightenment. Notwithstanding the missionary zeal of some moralist movements (maybe even because of them), the once popular banner line, "God is dead," is still a pervasive, if unconscious, current in a somewhat cynical Western world culture.

It was in this context that the publishing world was taken by surprise when a young monk's autobiography quickly became a bestseller. The Trappists and other religious orders were overwhelmed by the number of postulants to the monastic life who responded to his story. It was at the end of the 1940s that Thomas Merton shared his story with the world in The Seven Storey Mountain. From that time, until his death in 1968, he continued to write voluminously.

His writings on the life of the spirit, on prayer, contemplation and inner life, solitude, and mankind's alienation from, and possible reconciliation with God, never failed to strike a responsive chord in his diverse reading public. A monk's austere and demanding existence was apparently fertile ground which produced the fruits for which many hungered in the midst of their plenty.

It may be that the primary factor in the appeal of Merton's writings is his characteristic of penetrating in clear language to truth. His works lead the reader to a depth of self-understanding through a sharing of his own inner discoveries.

Merton's diligent study of Christian saints, mystics, and theologians was never expressed in his writings as a sterile erudition. The reader always gets the impression that "here is something alive," Merton is telling me something real, he is sharing profound discoveries that have significance for my life here in the 20th century. In the same way, his eremitic calling did not separate him from his fellow humans who toil in the world; he was not of the spiritual elite. The body of his published works chronicles a growing contact with the ground being, and he makes it clear that his inner life of the spirit is the heritage of all mankind.

Although there were many apparent obstacles to walking the path he perceived as being his path--that of a contemplative monk--all elements in his life added up to create in him a fully realized human being. His European beginnings, his wild youth and rebellious college days, his vocational self-doubt, the growing awareness that the mere form of monasticism was insufficient for his spiritual unfolding, the struggles with the Church censors over his writings, the prolonged delay in being allowed to go into hermitage, the demands placed upon a solitary monk by a world hungry for his words, the physical deprivations he had to suffer as the price of his hermitage, and, finally, the trip to the East and meetings with monks and spiritual leaders from non-Christian traditions--all contributed to the message he felt so naturally compelled to share with his fellow sojourners in the modern age.

He was a monk in a Christian religious order dating from the Middle Ages, yet he was a modern. He was a contemplative who treasured solitude, yet he knew this world very well and shared not only his "thoughts in solitude" but also his observations on contemporary times. His purpose among us was to report on the deepest meaning of human existence, and he did it with wit and humor and always with love.

Given the depth of his writings and the response they evoked in hundreds of thousands of his contemporaries, it should serve as a useful purpose to look at some of the factors that were involved in his awakening to the spiritual vocation.

Having arrived at the midpoint of his life, Thomas Merton made the decision to become a Trappist monk. This was not done on a whim nor was it an instantaneous conversion. In his autobiography, published when he was 32, he details some of the chance fortuitous events that prepared him for his spiritual vocation. His recognition of the importance of these occurrences was not always immediate. Nor was his response to them always appropriate for rapid spiritual unfolding. All that notwithstanding, they made their impact, and he arrived at "True North."

Merton's discovery of this vocation involved a process of self-recollection that was kindled by seemingly unimportant or irrelevant events. Some people consider such ultimately poignant encounters to be miracles, others consider them to be coincidence, while, for most people, these potential turning points in life go largely unnoticed or ignored. Merton himself came to view these unexpectedly fortuitous events as the work of grace. His awakening and the deepening inner life that followed during the last half of his life are attributable to the influence of a few of the people who crossed his path in the first half of his life. Part of that influence developed the character trait of being able to give up previously held beliefs quite readily when he grasped that they were in error. This seems to have become the way he related to the world and to his vocation: a way of humility and disattachment.

Spiritually fortuitous circumstances of his life began with his parents. His childhood was rich in experience as his parents moved frequently, living in Europe and the United States. Before Tom was born, his father had been tempted to join an Antarctic exploring expedition that passed through their town in France, but he did not go, and this "circumstance" resulted in Thomas' birth in 1925. His mother was a devout Quaker, yet she did not allow religion to "intrude" on her child's environment.

She consciously tried to keep from molding him according to her own ways. Merton's comment in his autobiography on this is probably accurate: "My guess is she thought, if I were left to myself I would grow up into a nice quiet Deist of some sort and never be perverted by superstition." An example of her singular approach to assure that her son thought for himself is the way she used her own death as a teaching for him. Thomas was six years old when she died, and she would not allow the child to see her in the hospital in the last few weeks. Instead, she wrote him a note telling him about what was happening which he read after her death. He was thus left to contemplate this major event in his life on his own and without the immediate emotional confusion that might have accompanied a closer participation.

His father was an artist and an independent man. He followed his vocation even though it meant a meager existence for his family. He taught Thomas that art was not for entertainment nor for the pleasure of the senses but that it was a means of contemplating the wholeness of creation. At age 11, Tom attended school at the Lycee Ingres at Montauban, France. Among the rough children there, he assumed the fashion of anti-Catholicism and anti-Semitism. But, characteristic of his quick intelligence, he shed those biases readily when he met Catholic youngsters who were much more refined in comparison with his classmates. He was already writing by this time, having written three romance novels with some of his schoolmates.

In the summer of 1927, he met Monsieur and Madame Privat, who were the people with whom he and his father boarded in Murat, France. Merton's description of them from The Seven Storey Mountain is that "they were saints in that most effective and telling way: sanctified by leading ordinary lives in a completely supernatural manner, sanctified by obscurity, by usual skills, by common tasks, by routine, but skills, tasks, routine which received a supernatural form from grace within, and from the habitual union of their souls with God in deep faith

39

and charity." The Privats were deeply concerned at young Merton's (age 12) lack of faith. Even though he argued with them that it was a matter for individual conscience, they did not contend with him. Later, he wrote that he owed much to them because of their prayers for him, perhaps he owed them even his religious vocation.

His freshman year, spent at Cambridge, was a dizzy and boisterous one. He felt the only thing of value that he got out of Cambridge was an acquaintance with Dante's works.

He returned to his maternal grandparents in Long Island and went to Columbia in the winter of 1935. Merton had been attracted at this time by the Socialists who were on campus. He relished the idea of a classless society. His course selection the next year reflected this intellectual social-political concern. One day, thinking he was in the room where the first meeting of his history course was to be held, he found that it was actually a course on Shakespeare and he started to leave. But, just by chance, he reconsidered, and ended up taking the course. It was this "coincidence" that led to his friendship with Professor Van Doren. Merton was immediately impressed with the "heroic humility" of his English professor. Van Doren was one of several people at Columbia who influenced him in the direction of using the mind to penetrate the meaning of things through perfect honesty and objectivity. From Van Doren, Merton was weaned from the narrow perspective of philosophy and economics through studying Shakespeare, which dealt with human drama in the fundamental realms of life, death, sorrow, and eternity. It was also in this class that Merton became acquainted with Bob Lax, who became his good friend and was to have a pivotal influence on his life.

Merton describes Lax as being born a great contemplative. He had a deep spirituality but, lacking practicality, he followed Merton's lead in activities. It was Bob Lax who inspired Merton with the desire to read Aldous Huxley's Ends and Means. In the entry for November 27, 1941, The Secular Journal of Thomas Merton, Merton declares, "until I read this book, Ends and Means, four years ago, I had never much heard of the word mysticism. The part he played in my conversion, by that book, was very great." The main thrust of the book was that evil means will not accomplish good ends. One needs detachment in order to act with conscious will rather than be subject to the inferior material and animal forces of one's nature. Asceticism and prayer are the means to freedom.

For Merton this was revolutionary. He was not yet ready to end his playboy ways. Indeed, as a result of being so busy with his various forms of socializing, he became seriously ill.

It was also through his friendship with Bob Lax that he encountered a shy little man with a huge smile, a yellow turban with Hindu prayers written all over it in red, and, on his feet, sneakers. Bramachari was his name, and he earned Merton's respect quickly by his good humor and his inability to criticize in a judgmental way, even when making statements about the hyprocrisy of most western sects. When Merton told Bramachari of his difficulty in relating to the eastern mysticism he had studied as a result of Huxley's book, Bramachari referred him to the beautiful Christian mystical tradition. He specifically told Merton he should read St. Augustine's Confes-

sions and The Imitation of Christ by St. Ignatius.
Aside from putting Merton in touch with the western
mystical tradition, Bramachari left an impression on
him that contributed to Merton's eventual preoccupation with bridging the dogmatic chasm which the
western traditions have maintained against the
"heathen" creeds.

Merton felt the call to a spiritual vocation with
increasing intensity in his last year as an undergraduate. He was drawn to the Catholic Mass and had an
intimate feeling for the mystical body of the Church.
He had just suffered a personal life crisis, and all his
activities drained him to the point of exhaustion. At
one point in his reading of Lahey's Life of Gerard
Manley Hopkins, the questions in the text asking the
reason for Hopkin's hesitation about converting to
Catholicism seemed to be a movement within
himself, Merton, a voice moving him to take the
decision he knew he must. He went into the street
and to the church where he had obtained some books,
and told the priest he wanted to become a Catholic.
A few months after his baptism, he realized that he
was living in the same manner as he had before
baptism. He pleased himself before all else, all his
acts interfering with the work of grace in his soul.
His "conversion" consisted in an intellectual change
only.

The state of the world at the end of the 1930s,
no less than the state of his own soul, led Merton to a
vocational crisis. As he and Lax were walking down
the street arguing about something, Lax asked Tom
what he wanted to be anyway. Thomas responded not
that he wanted to be a well-known book reviewer for
the New York Times, or a successful businessman, or
some such profession, but he said that he wanted to

be a good Catholic. Unable to explain what he meant by that, he was told by Lax that what he should say is that he wanted to be a saint. Merton protested, asking how it would be possible for him to be a saint. Lax, who was not a Catholic, remarked that all that is necessary to be a saint is to want to be one.

By September of that year, Merton was thinking, "I am going to be a priest." One evening, he went to a church service, feeling that he was called there to answer a question and that his whole life depended on his decision. Thus, he answered in prayer: "Yes, I want to be a priest, with all my heart I want it. If it is Your will, make me a priest." He wrote about these prayers in his autobiography: "When I had said them, I realized in some measure what I had done with those last four words, what power I had put into motion on my behalf, and what union had been sealed between me and that power by my decision."

However, it was a few years before his decision was actualized. He talked to people about his vocation and investigated several religious orders in the Catholic Church. He decided upon the Franciscan order. Within a few weeks of entering the novitiate, he was beset with many anguished doubts. He spoke with the superior, expressing his concern that his past life made him unworthy. His superior suggested that he withdraw his application. Was he to be excluded from the priesthood? For a long time, he was unable to speak to anyone about his vocation, but his attitude and behavior changed after this. Ironically, when he doubted the very existence of his vocation he began moving closer to it.

At last, in December, 1941, he entered the Cistercian Trappist monastery at Gethsemani, Kentucky, taking vows of Stability, Obedience, and

Conversion of Life; thus, undertaking a life in the strictest of the monastic orders in the Catholic Church.

For one who had been a rebel all his life, obedience would seem to be the hardest of the vows to live up to. But the others, too, were at extreme odds with the temperment he had shown for 26 years. He was put to the test of his vows during most of the next 27 years of his life.

For example, he continued to have a weak constitution and was sick for long periods, yet he never left the strict routine of the monastery or complained. And, he had to wait many years before he was allowed to follow his vocation of solitude in hermitage. He was faithful to his vow of Obedience by accepting the function of Master of Novices at Gethsemani and fulfilling the responsibilities of that office for ten years, all the while yearning for the complete solitude that was his calling. He joked about this situation but never complained about it. He finally was allowed his hermitage if he would build it himself. The construction was stopped short when the Abbot saw the solid little structure he had established; community life was the norm at Gethsemani and Merton's eremiticism might be too appealing. So, his cabin had only a small fireplace for heat against the harsh Kentucky winters. Even though sickly, Merton did not complain during the three years he spent in hermitage there. He found his solitude.

It is more than interesting to note that the succeeding Abbot himself made use of the hermitage and that the ermitic is once again a respected vocation among the Cistercians.

During those three years, Merton deepened his spiritual search, especially his studies in Zen which he had begun seriously in the late 1950s. He continued to write, and much of his correspondence was extensive and worldwide. One of those with whom he corresponded was Dr. D. T. Suzuki, the Zen authority. Merton became more and more conversant with the Eastern religions. He had even undertaken to learn Chinese, but the pressure of his other work made him give it up. He read voraciously all the books supplied to him by various sources--librarian friends, Dr. Paul K. T. Sih (who supplied him with the Legge translation of Chinese Classics), and other scholars. One of his close brothers at Gethsemani, Patrick Hart, comments that Merton's growing knowledge and interest in the East was clearly "providential preparation" for his Asian trip. As with Merton's other realizations and understanding, he had shared his discoveries about Eastern thought with the reading public through numerous books on various topics: The Way of Chuang Tzu, Zen and the Birds of Appetite, Mystics and Zen Masters, The Significance of the Bhagavad Gita. According to Dr. Suzuki, Merton had become one of the few Westerners who really understood Zen.

Merton was drawn to his studies in Eastern mysticism and religion and understood them so well because of his intimate affinity for, understanding, and personal experience of the mystical tradition of his own Christian heritage. At any rate, by August of 1968, he was engaged in planning for his trip to Asia. He had received permission to travel away from Gethsemani (a dispensaton from the rule that a monk does not leave his monastery because of his vow of stability) to attend a fall conference in Bangkok organized by a Benedictine group aiming for monastic renewal. The conference was to be a gathering of all Asian monastic leaders, and Merton had been invited to deliver one of the principal addresses. This trip was the culmination and fulfillment of his studies of the Eastern traditions. His itinerary included visits to many Buddhist monasteries as well as Christian missions. He accepted another invitation to speak at an interfaith Spiritual Summit Conference in Calcutta shortly before the Bangkok meeting and also hoped to be able to meet with the Dalai Lama and other Eastern religious leaders.

The publication of his journal kept while he traveled throughout Asia on that occasion, The Asian Journal of Thomas Merton, reveals his excited enthusiasm in encountering not only the leaders but the monks, the countryside, the hermits, and the teachings. It is evident that he continued reading during the trip; there are numerous entries in the journal summarizing thoughts and quoting from texts of various different religious approaches to the spiritual life. In it we also learn firsthand the insights he gained from the people and places he encountered along the way. This material reveals why his ecumenicism was so comprehensive of all religious traditions.

Immediately after delivering his talk entitled "Marxism and Monastic Perspectives" in Bangkok on December 10, 1968, Thomas Merton died of an accidental electrocution in his hotel room. Thus, his life had begun in Europe and ended in Asia. The first 26 years were spent in a healthy worldliness through which he learned disattachment to his belief structures and renouncement of his outmoded ways of relating to the world and his own life. The last 27 years were spent in applying that same renouncement in fulfilling the vows he had made as a member of the Trappists and in realizing his unique individual way to meet the divine. He died in the East that he had come to know through its mysticism, his last actions involving efforts to bridge the East-West chasm that his own understanding had transcended.

Overall, Merton's life has meaning for us--it brings us The Message. His written work rings with authenticity, almost continuously, like a bell: clear, precise, unadorned. His words announce again and again the truth of man's union with divine spirit. The radiance of his work emanates from the essential message of his life: in a continuous process of perfecting his relationship to the divine, Merton disappears. His life was a work which transformed the man into the message.

Paradoxically, his work of perfecting humility brought this solitary contemplative to the attention of a vast public. His clear revelations about the spiritual and mystical life answered an apparent need of mid-20th century Western man.

But, the full extent of his practical self-effacement is not readily noticed in his writing. He removes himself so effectively that even in his numerous journals, it is the voice of all mankind that speaks from them. We learn remarkably little about his personal life.

It seems that the personal dimension had very low priority in his life. This reveals something about the way he related to his vows. As a Cistercian monk, his vows are probably summed up in the vow of Conversion of Life. Merton made of this vow a living reality--disappearing as a separate personality and transforming his life into a testament to the living spirit.

47

It would be no more than speculation to talk of what Merton would have done with his life and his writing talent if he had not entered the Cistercian Order or had not persevered in fulfilling his strict vows. What is certain, though, is that through fidelity to his vocation and the humility that nourished his spiritual insight, his writing was focused on answering the spiritual needs of a disoriented modern age.

He disappeared and, in the process of that transformation, he left The Message.

Based on the presentation by Gordon Waters.
Opening quotation from the September 1968 Circular Letter to Friends, quoted by Brother Patrick Hart in his Foward to The Asian Journal of Thomas Merton.

References and Recommended Readings

These four books by Thomas Merton should be considered essential reading by any seeker or aspiring contemplative.

The Seven Storey Mountain. New York: Harcourt,
    Brace and Company, 1948.
    Thoroughly enjoyable and engaging autobiography of the young monk, revealing the power of the discerning heart to transform a life; the epilogue is especially powerful and perhaps prophetic.

New Seeds of Contemplation. New York: New
    Directions, 1962.
    Meditative essays in an almost poetic prose;
gives clear exposition of many of the dimensions
of spiritual life. It is intended mainly for people
without formal religious ties, although it has a
noticeable Christian and Catholic perspective
which should not be a hindrance for even
non-Christians.

Thoughts in Solitude. New York: Farrar, Straus, and
    Giroux, 1956.
    Considered by Merton to be fundamental
thoughts on the contemplative life, written during special periods when he was afforded the
opportunity to meditate in solitude.

The Asian Journal of Thomas Merton. New York:
    New Directions, 1973.
    Literally the last word. This is Thomas Merton
at his height--the journal he kept while traveling
to two spiritual conferences, one in Calcutta and
the other in Bangkok (where he died following his
talk). It is a rich and stimulating record of his
encounter with monks and mysticism of the East
at firsthand. Replete with photographs taken by
Thomas Merton, it records his thoughts, the
teachings he received from other spiritual masters like the Dalai Lama, Nyaponika Thera,
Trungpa Rimpoche, etc., excerpts from written
explanations of Eastern religious traditions and
their teachings (thoroughly footnoted by the
editors), with a glossary, appendices, and the
written texts of his Calcutta and Bangkok talks.

Merton's journals are very good; two early ones are:

The Sign of Jonas. New York: Harcourt, Brace and Company, 1953.

Conjectures of a Guilty Bystander. New York: Doubleday, 1966.

Translations and selections made by Thomas Merton are instructive, enjoyable, and accurate. Some highly recommended examples are:

The Wisdom of the Desert: Sayings from the Desert Fathers of the Fourth Century. New York: New Directions, 1970.
One of Merton's own favorites, introduces one to a neglected Christian mysticism not unlike that of the Zen Masters of Japan and China.

Gandhi on Nonviolence. New York: New Directions, 1973.
A powerful selection arranged under headings, with a moving introduction by Merton commenting on the demented pursuit of atomic superiority by modern nations.

Collections of Merton's works and books about him are many and increasing. There is some danger of getting an arrangement of his thoughts that distorts the message, but the following titles are recommended:

The Man in the Sycamore Tree. By Ed Rice.
  An excellent biography, very light-hearted and
  humorous. One gets the feeling of knowing
  Thomas Merton the man. Many interesting facts
  and some speculations you will not find else-
  where.

The Solitary Explorer. By Elena Malits. New York:
  Harper and Row, 1980.
  Another fine biography that relates Merton's
  spiritual development, his writings, and historical events together. It is a guide to Merton's
  life and writings by a woman who know the inner
  life. She characterizes his life as one of "continuous conversion."

Thomas Merton on Mysticism. By Raymond Bailey.
  New York: Doubleday, 1975.

Thomas Merton on Peace. Fine introduction by
  Gordon C. Zahn. McCall Publishing Company,
  1971.

Poetry:

The Geography of Lograire
Cables to the Ace
Original Child Bomb
Raids on the Unspeakable
Selected Poems. Introduction by Mark Van Doren.

Other:

A Hidden Wholeness. By Thomas Merton and John
  Howard Griffen. Houghton Mifflin, 1970. A
  collection of photographs.

Bibliography. By Frank Dell'Isola. Farrar, Straus, and Cudahy, 1956.

_____. By Marquite Breit (through 1956-1974). Scarecrow Press, 1974.

The Oakland Public Library has tape recordings of Thomas Merton addressing the Center for the Study of Democratic Institutions in Santa Barbara, California, before departing on his journey to the East.

DOROTHY DAY
Worker

*We cannot love God unless we love each
other, and to love we must know each
other . . . . We have all known the long
loneliness and we have learned that the
only solution is love and that love comes
with community.*

The most recent edition of the autobiography,
The Long Loneliness, has a picture on the cover of
Dorothy Day in old age walking through the woods in
the fall. The publisher's subtitle at the bottom of the
picture calls her book, "The Story of the Greatest
Woman of Our Time." This is quite a statement to
make, but it is particularly interesting because
Dorothy Day is not exactly a household name. But,
she is well-known in certain circles, especially among
people who are trying to do the same kind of work
that she did.

Since her death at the age of 83 in November of
1980, there has been a renewed interest in the work
of Dorothy Day and her philosophy. Many articles
have been written about her ideas, often by the
people who knew her and worked with her. In an
interview published last year, the Argentine who
received the Nobel Peace Prize, Adolfo Perez

Equivel, said that in order to learn about peace, we need to study the life of Dorothy Day. He included also the lives of Mahatma Gandhi, Martin Luther King, and Thomas Merton. What all these people shared in common was their philosophy of nonviolence. Dorothy Day was a social reformer who believed that our social problems could and had to be resolved nonviolently. But, she did not always think this way. Her life, if anything, was a life of change. She was a radical and a Communist in her early youth, later converted to Catholicism and took the Christian message of love to heart in her work for the poor and the workers. A look at her life and the changes in her thinking documents this development of her world view of peace and nonviolence.

Dorothy Day was born in 1897 in Brooklyn, New York. Her father was a Calvinist and a firm believer in the Protestant Work Ethic. Her mother was Episcopalian, and it was in this church that Dorothy was first baptised and confirmed. For all the years she was growing up, her father worked as a newspaperman, and this affected the family in a number of ways. For one thing, they moved a lot, so Dorothy often found herself in new situations and having to make new friends. Her father also worked nights and slept days, so the children had to be quiet in order not to disturb his sleep. To occupy themselves quietly throughout the days, the children read a great deal, and from a very early age they wrote stories, essays, and even created a family newspaper. This was to mark the beginning of Dorothy's later career as a writer.

When she was six years old, the family moved to California, living first in Berkeley and eventually settling in Oakland. Her most vivid memory of their

life in the Bay Area was of the big San Francisco
earthquake in 1906. She remembers being awakened
in the early morning hours by a roar in the earth and
the sensation that the roof was going to cave in.
Their house was cracked from roof to floor, many
things were broken, but no one in the house was hurt.
The next day, hundreds of refugees from the City
came across the Bay, seeking shelter in the less-
damaged East Bay. Dorothy found something that
she liked very much in all this activity. She liked the
way in which everyone was so kind and loving to
those less fortunate than themselves, and she felt for
the first time the joy of doing good for others. The
Oakland residents very generously gave away their
food and clothing, and her mother cooked pots and
pots of soup. Dorothy realized that human beings
could be truly good and unselfish. And, she looked
back on this example from her childhood as a reminder and as an inspiration over her long life of
service to the poor and suffering.

Because of the earthquake, her father's newspaper company burned to the ground and he lost his
job. The family moved to Chicago to find work. In
between trying to write a novel, Mr. Day did odd
jobs, and the family lived for several years on a very
meager income. They lived in the working class
neighborhood not far from the factories, and the
families of hard-working industrial workers made up
her new companions. For the first time, Dorothy
became acquainted with Catholics, for many Poles,
Italians, and Irish workers lived in these Chicago
neighborhoods. Her next-door neighbors were a
family of nine children. She played over at their
house often, and their mother used to tell the children the stories of the lives of the saints. Dorothy

went back to her own house and asked her mother
why they never prayed or sang hymns in their home.
And her mother was rather at odds about how to deal
with this pious little girl.

One day, Dorothy went running through the
house of her neighbors, looking for her playmates,
and ran, by accident, into their mother's room. The
mother was kneeling and praying. A rush of love and
gratitude and happiness flashed through little
Dorothy at this sight, an emotion that she was never
to forget. She was moved by the love of God of this
woman seen through this simple act of prayer.
Religion, for the young girl, had authority and meaning at this stage in her life. She had the simple faith
of a child. There were no questions, no doubts. She
herself longed to become a saint and wrote stories on
how to do so with her young Catholic friends.

At the age of 15, Dorothy read for the first time
a book that was to change her life, Upton Sinclair's
The Jungle. It was a book about the frightening
factory conditions in Chicago at that time, and it
opened her eyes to the life of Chicago around her.
She would walk the streets and neighborhoods of her
city and think about the characters in this book, and
she felt somehow that her life was linked with theirs.
She was moved by the suffering of her neighbors and
friends who gave so much of themselves to their
horrendously difficult and dangerous factory jobs.
She writes in her autobiography that she received "a
call, a vocation, a direction to my life" through this
book, wanting from that time on to devote her life to
helping the poor and the workers.

At age 16, she received a scholarship to go to
the University of Illinois, having scholastically sur-
passed all the other pupils in the county school

district. She was very happy to leave home, looking for adventure. She did not really have plans to study anything in particular, but she was, she writes, seeking experience. She was young and the world was waiting for her. And her schooling was to lead to a fierce desire within herself to radically change many things about the world.

While at college, she read books that inspired her: Dostoevsky, Tolstoy, and the worker stories of Jack London. These books added to her interest in working conditions, and she became absorbed with the idea of radicalism and the class war. She sought friends who shared the same interests, joining a group of young Socialists on campus. Her favorite slogan at this time became the Marxist slogan, "Workers of the world unite! You have nothing to lose but your chains!" and she would shout this whenever the situation availed itself, much to the consternation of her parents at the dinner table.

The philosophy of Dostoevsky and Tolstoy made her cling to her faith, but her new interest in workers' problems seemed in contradiction to her old religious feelings. Religion seemed to preach meekness and peace and joy, but there was so much suffering in the world that needed to be changed. She did not want to be meek, she wanted a revolution. And being religious seemed to interfere with this. One of her professors said that we should remember that religion throughout the ages brought comfort to many people. She interpreted this to mean that people who were weak needed religion. And she wasn't weak, she was strong! So, she pushed, very consciously, all religious feeling from her heart. Religion, after all, was the opiate of the people.

After two years at the university, she left to become a full-time reporter on the Marxist paper, The Call. The year was 1915. There had been some changes in working conditions. Many places now had the ten-hour work day, and there had been some advance in the hourly wage. But, there was still so much work to be done, and there was a great hope among young people that they would change the world. Dorothy became attracted to the IWW at this time--the International Workers of the World, or the Wobblies as they are more often called. Their idea was that one great union of the workers of the world would eventually solve the world's problems. They believed in direct action--organized unions, strikes, and pickets. They were perhaps the most passionate of the labor groups, very dedicated and organized. A real folklore developed around them, and they even had a book of songs which added to their appeal and ability to inspire. "The Little Red Songbook," as it was affectionately called, was written "to fan the flames of discontent" among workers of their unfair and unsafe working conditions. Like the Marxists, the Wobblies thought religion was used by the rich to subjugate the poor. Themes from their songs often reflect this view. There is one famous song with the line: "You'll get pie in the sky when you die." In other words, the rich tell the poor workers not to complain, to be good, to be pious and humble about their lot in the world, and when they die they will go to heaven and find all the comforts they could ever want. The group refrain in response to this reasoning is sung with vigor: "It's a lie!" The revolutionaries of the time felt that religion was used as a means of justifying the great injustices waged against workers, and so, rejected all forms of it. They imagined a world free from hunger and suffering, where one did not have to rely on God. The workers' union was everything.

Dorothy lived the life of a radical bohemian in New York during the early 1920s. She was constantly writing, working for the Communist paper, The Masses, and trying to write The Great Novel, as were so many young idealists in the city at that time. She belonged to a group of young intellectuals who shared artistic and political ideals, and through them came to know Eugene O'Neil, Harte Crane, and even Trotsky. All of her friends were either Communists, Socialists, or Wobblies. She stayed out late every night in discussion at local cafes, walking the streets of New York, and singing songs of revolution.

On March 21, 1917, she joined in the momentous celebration in Madison Square Garden where thousands rejoiced in the victory of the workers in the Russian Revolution. All that hungered for economic justice saw the revolution as a "cry for world peace and brotherhood."

That same year, Dorothy was arrested and jailed for the first of 12 such occasions in her life. She went to the White House to picket for women's voting rights and was arrested with 35 other suffragettes of all ages. At their trial, the leaders were given six months imprisonment, the older women 15 days, and all the others--herself included--30 days. As soon as the verdict was declared, the women announced that they would go on a hunger strike. A most moving rendition of the suffering they endured is found in the chapter entitled, "Jail," in her autobiography. For ten days they ate nothing, using their twice-a-day visit to the hallway bathroom to drink as much hot water as they could to ease the hollow pain in their stomachs. A few of the older women grew sick, and the officers in charge force fed them with hoses down their throats. The press got a hold of the story, and the attention that it raised was not good for the court's position. The strikers were all released on the 11th day. But Dorothy was never to forget the deep sense of desolation that she felt as she lay alone all day and night in her cell. Never had she felt so alone, and never had their cause seemed so hopeless to her. She had endless hours to think about the suffering and the plight of all human beings and found that she could find solace in no thought on her own. A guardsman gave her a copy of the Bible, and she found comfort in the lofty human spirit of the Psalms. She began to think that maybe human beings needed help from a source higher than themselves and that there were times when the spirit of the workers' union was not enough.

When Dorothy was 26, she fell in love. He was a young revolutionary like herself, an anarchist as well as an atheist. He loved nature more than anything, and he supported himself by fishing and odd jobs. They lived together in a bungalow by the ocean, he working, she writing. When Dorothy writes of her time spent with him, she refers to him as her husband, though they never did legally marry. They considered marriage to be a thing of the establishment and too bourgeois. They were together for several years and had a child.

His influence on her life was something of an irony, for it certainly would not have been what he intended. He loved nature and creation so much, Dorothy writes, that he inspired in her a love for the Creator. She was often in awe of his relationship with the sea, the outdoors, his garden. Through him she saw so much beauty in the world that she again felt her younger yearnings to know more about the beginnings and creation of all life. She felt an overwhelming need to love God who had created a world that she grew to love so much. Natural happiness with the man she loved brought her to the love of the supernatural. Her husband could not understand her renewed interest in spiritual matters and interpreted her intentions as nothing more than that of an irrational woman. She found herself even going to Sunday Mass at a nearby country church, and this caused a great deal of conflict between the couple.

When her daughter was born, Dorothy's spiritual desires grew more intense, and she declared to raise her child within a life that incorporated the spiritual. She felt that the greatest gift she could give to her daughter was the gift of faith. In her autobiography, she said: "I was not going to have her floundering through many years as I had, doubting and hesitating, undisciplined and amoral." Dorothy began reading in order to find answers to the questions she was asking about life, finding especially inspiring William James' The Varieties of Religious Experience and The Imitation of Christ by St. Ignatius. She spent many hours talking to a kindly old nun who lived near her church, and she eventually decided to have herself and her child baptised.

This decision would have its high costs, and Dorothy knew this. But, her new love for the spiritual was so great that it could not be denied. After her child's baptism, the father of her child left them. Dorothy's life was to take an entirely new direction.

Dorothy continued to pursue her interest in writing, finding in it an outlet for the difficult period of loneliness that she was going through as a young, single parent. She went to Mexico for several months to do journalistic research and acquired there some distance from her former life which helped her overcome her sorrow. She also wrote a novel which had minor commercial success. It was read by a Hollywood producer who wanted to make a movie of it. Dorothy was hired to go to Los Angeles to oversee the production of the film and to do editing of screenplays. She went eagerly to California, anticipating many good, new changes. But, she did not find the kind of work she really wanted to do and ended up moving back to New York within a few short months.

There, she supported herself doing various freelance jobs, writing mostly for Catholic publications, especially for the Jesuit magazine, The Commonweal. Throughout this period, she maintained her interest in the labor movement and in liberal causes, but she began to feel a distance from some of her former associates. They regarded her conversion to Catholicism as something very peculiar indeed and had no understanding of her desire for a spiritual life. A real break with her old way of life occurred when Dorothy went to Washington to cover a Communist rally. Throughout the march, Dorothy was struck by the distance between her philosophy and the Communist ideology. She was a Catholic now and there were fundamental differences in the two systems of thought. She knew that she was no longer one of them, and yet, she loved their zeal and their nonselfish desire to help the poor and the suffering. She felt that her work as a Catholic until then had been selfish and personal, a time of solitary reading and introspection. And here she saw her Communist brothers in struggle, not for themselves, but for others. She longed to find a way to blend her love for the Catholic religion with her love for social work. She went to the national shrine at the Catholic University that night to offer a special prayer, "a prayer which came with tears and with anguish, that some way would open for me to use what talents I possessed for my fellow workers, for the poor." And when she arrived back in New York, she found the answer to her prayers.

Waiting for her was Peter Maurin--Peter, the French peasant--whose spirit and ideas were to dominate the rest of her life. He was a short, stocky man in his mid-50s, as ragged and rugged as any marching worker that she had ever encountered. She liked him immediately. He explained to Dorothy that the editor of The Commonweal had told him to come and see her, because, it was said, "We think alike." And, think alike they did. Their conversation that day was to lead to a lifelong collaboration and mutual admiration. Peter had a vision, an idea for a society "where it is easier for men to be good." And, he wanted to engage Dorothy in his plan for a better world.

Peter Maurin wanted to create an organization of Catholics who were concerned with the problems of the working poor. This group would center around many activities, including round-table discussions where ideas were generated, houses of hospitality where direct help to the poor could be given, and a newspaper which would spread ideas throughout the country. Dorothy thought these were all very good ideas, and it is amazing how, within a few short months of their acquaintance, everything fell into place. Since Dorothy was the writer, she took over the newspaper, with Peter Maurin as chief advisor. A few young college students started in on the plan, and together they raised money for a first issue of their paper, which at first was going to be called The Catholic Radical and which became The Catholic Worker. The first issue came out on May Day, 1933, the traditional Workers' Day. Dorothy and a few volunteers went into Union Square to sell their paper for one penny a copy, giving reading access to even the poorest of workers. In Union Square stood representatives of all the various radical groups, from the Communists to the Wobblies, while off to one corner the enthusiastic Catholic Workers shouted the virtues of their paper. The reds were, no doubt, amazed to see Catholics out among them, but much to their surprise, the paper really attracted attention. The first issue of 2,500 copies sold out immediately, and within three months The Catholic Worker sold subscriptions to 25,000 readers. Within three years, the circulation was 150,000. The basic social philosophy of this paper was striking a responsive cord among Catholic and non-Catholic workers alike.

The social philosophy held by The Catholic Worker differed from some of the other worker movements of the time. They held the philosophy of rigid pacifism, which included opposition to war as well as a rejection of the violent revolutionary class struggle. They also had an acceptance of private property, finding that owning and working one's own land was an important need for human beings. And, they believed that the less government interference the better; more important than government hand-outs was the guarantee of a job. Their slogan was

64

"Work not wages," for work to them was vital to human dignity. They highly valued manual labor as well, recognizing that no matter how industrial the world would become, there would always be work that needed to be done by hand.

The Catholic Workers grew strong as a group, attracting many volunteers as their paper expanded. They incorporated into their work a means of "direct action" for the poor, which was comprised of houses of hospitality in almost every major city of the country, giving shelter to the homeless and soup to the hungry. Twelve farms were established which provided food for the houses and where Catholic familes had the opportunity to leave the world for a few days at a time to recollect and reevaluate their lives.

The spiritual life was always basic to the approach of Dorothy Day, and her regular column, "On Pilgrimage," was full of her beautiful observations and discoveries. To live, said Dorothy, was to be on pilgrimage. But the journey of life was not always an easy one. Life, Dorothy recognized, was "the long loneliness," but it was a loneliness that could be endured. The solution was love--love for the poor, the tired, the hungry, the suffering of the world. It was the love found in the Catholic idea of the Mystical Body of Christ, the recognition that in each and every human being was the reflection of the divine nature of Christ.

From their very beginning, The Catholic Worker maintained their editorial stance of absolute nonviolence, and this extended even throughout World War II, a war which most people found justifiable. Dorothy Day wrote many articles during this period about the need for nonviolent action in dealing with world conflicts. The Catholic Workers, for example, were among the first groups to protest the German embassy for the Nazi regime's treatment of the Jews. But going to war was another matter. Christians have always believed in the commandment, Thou shalt not kill, and yet they have always found justifications for not following it. Dorothy Day felt that it was vital for the world to reach the point where we would have no compromise about war. Nonviolence, according to Dorothy Day, was "the acceptance of suffering." Suffering, especially unjust suffering, when endured as an offering, has a transforming effect on the world; it creates a force, an energy, as did Christ's unjust death. But people could not understand this mystical approach to suffering, and The Catholic Worker lost thousands of subscriptions during World War II. There were times when Dorothy wondered if they should have maintained their hard editorial line. She recognized that people were not ready to hear what they had to say. She wrote in The Long Loneliness: "We have always acknowledged the primacy of the spiritual, and to have undertaken a life of silence, manual labor, and prayer might have been the better way."

In the sixties, the Catholic Workers were early in their protest of the Vietnam War and became advisors for the growing antiwar sentiment. They were also a major part of farm labor protests, and Dorothy Day herself was in many a march with Caesar Chavez and the United Farm Workers.

The houses of hospitality, retreat houses, and farms are found throughout the country today, and The Catholic Worker newspaper remains the best-priced paper at still only one penny a copy. It is interesting to ponder the changes that came about in

a young woman's life that led to such a transform-
ation--Dorothy Day transformed not only herself but
all those lives that she touched. And Dorothy Day
touched thousands. Her spirit will be with us always,
for she left in her writings not only the solitary voice
of one passionate, idealistic woman, but also the
cries of all those who suffer and labor in the world,
the poor and the workers.

Based on the presentation by Patricia K. Colleran.
Opening quotation from Dorothy Day, The Long
Loneliness.

References and Recommended Readings

Day, Dorothy. From Union Square to Rome. Silver
    Spring, Maryland: Preservation of the Faith
    Press, 1940.

_____. Loaves and Fishes. New York: Harper and
    Row, 1963.

_____. The Long Loneliness. New York: Harper
    and Row, 1981.

_____. Meditations. New York: Newman Press,
    1970.

_____. On Pilgrimage: The Sixties. New York:
    Curtis Books, 1972.

MAHATMA GANDHI
Soul Force

> *But the path of self-purification is hard
> and steep. To attain to perfect purity one
> has to become absolutely passion-free in
> thought, speech and action; to rise above
> the opposing currents of love and hatred,
> attachment and repulsion . . . . To
> conquer the subtle passions seems to me
> to be far harder than the physical con-
> quest of the world by the force of arms.*

The popular image of Mahatma Gandhi is one of
a small, brown-skinned Indian dressed only in a
loincloth and sandles. And yet, this humble and
simple man was one of the greatest leaders the world
has ever seen. He was a man of extraordinary inner
strength who led the struggle in India for freedom
from British rule. His strength came not from
amassing wealth or commanding armies but from an
infinitely greater force, that of truth and nonviolence. The principles of truth and nonviolence--or
Satyagraha and Ahimsa--by which Gandhi lived his
life are of utmost importance to humanity today. In
a world where violence persists in our collective
unconscious, where brutality occurs daily, where progress poisons our environment, where most of our

creative energy is devoted to making extraordinarily destructive weapons, Gandhi's words of peace are rare and refreshing.

Mohandas Gandhi was born on October 2, 1869, in Porobander in western India. He was the fourth and last child in a family that was a member of the Hindu merchant caste. His father was a politician, and his mother--though illiterate--was a devoutly religious woman. As a child, Mohandas was very shy and had few friends. As a student, he was lazy and undisciplined, spending much of his time daydreaming. And, as a young adolescent, he had a very rebellious stage where he broke Hindu customs by smoking and eating meat. His early life is in contrast with the discipline and renouncement of his later adult years.

At the age of 13, Mohandas was married to another 13-year-old named Kasterbai in a prearranged agreement. Child marriage was common in India at this time, a practice that Gandhi was to protest in his later life. As a teenage husband, Gandhi was jealous and overprotective. He insisted that he was the decision maker of the house, often not letting his wife play outside with the other neighbor children. This was his way of dominating her.

When he finished school, Gandhi decided to study law in London. His father had died when he was 15, and Gandhi needed the approval of his mother to go so far away from home. She strongly resisted his plan to go, and consented only after her son took a vow not to touch wine, women, or meat.

He spent three years in London, leaving his young wife back in India. In England, Gandhi felt the conflict of the foreigner in a new land. On one hand, he tried to become English by dressing formally and adopting proper and genteel behavior. On the other hand, he retained his Indian personality by participating in a vegetarian society where he met fellow Indians and began to read the Bhagivad Gita for the first time. The Gita had such a great impact on Gandhi that it was to become his permanent companion, advisor, and spiritual source.

After completing his law studies and returning to India in 1891, Gandhi began a frustrating effort to establish a law practice. Because he was still very shy and had difficulties expressing himself in court, he was not yet able to fully represent his clients with the assertiveness necessary for an advocate. He had a particularly frustrating encounter when he tried to smooth out a conflict between his brother and a bureaucrat who blocked his promotion. Gandhi tried to reason with the man but was unsuccessful and ended up leaving in disgust. The man's pettiness and arrogance was characteristic of the small government domains throughout India, and this experience led Gandhi away from pursuing a career in government service.

Shortly thereafter, he accepted an offer to work as a lawyer in South Africa, where he was to represent Indians who had come as laborers. He arrived in South Africa in 1893. Not long after his arrival there, Gandhi came face to face with the racial discrimination that his fellow Indians submitted to daily.

During one of his cases, he was traveling with a first-class ticket on an overnight train to Pretoria. Midway in the journey, he was asked to leave his compartment because, as a brown-skinned man, he was not allowed to travel first class. He stubbornly refused to leave his seat and accept a lesser one and was eventually thrown off the train at the station in Maritzburg. He spent the rest of the night outside shivering and brooding over this degrading and humiliating experience. Never before had he been forced to face the full brunt of racism.

This event was significant in Gandhi's life in that it transformed and strengthened him. He was able to transcend his personal suffering and identify with the suffering of people everywhere who were oppressed and exploited. That night, Gandhi dedicated himself to the uprooting of injustice in the world. He would work to eliminate social, racial, and religious barriers that separated people from one another.

Gandhi had discovered an inner resolve and a new sense of purpose in his life. He was becoming more aware of an inner vocation that called him to make a deeper commitment with his life. In identifying with the suffering of others, Gandhi expanded spiritually. He was able to go beyond his own concerns and see the possibility of offering his life to a higher purpose.

Another significant event in Gandhi's life was his reading of Unto This End, a book about simplicity by the English writer, John Ruskin. This book had such a powerful influence on Gandhi that he changed his whole way of living. From then on, he embraced manual work as an expression of love for humanity. He could no longer place himself above any kind of labor. He took upon himself the work that had been previously done by others, especially by the untouchables, the lowest Hindu caste. He participated with all of humanity by consciously choosing to live in a more humble and simple way and thereby sharing the life that so many in the world are destined to live.

Gandhi's life of simplicity was a healthy one. He began to walk great distances to and from work each day. Walking became an important and much loved part of his daily routine, a time to reflect and contemplate.

A major change in Gandhi's life was his commitment to self-reliance. He began cutting his own hair and starching his own collars. He laughed along with those who teased him but persisted in his efforts until he became quite skilled.

As Gandhi became more committed to his new way of living, his shyness disappeared. He was more open and willing to experiment with his life without fearing failure or rejection by others.

In order to further develop some of these new ideas, Gandhi established a communal farm in South Africa based on simple living, self-sufficiency, and nonviolence. When he later returned to India, he continued to live in similar communities. For centuries the Indians have had the idea of living in such spiritual communities, or ashrams, and Gandhi expanded their philosophy to include the study of nonviolence.

The outward changes in Gandhi's life corresponded to a transformation that was occurring inwardly as well. As he was becoming more aware of his vocation, a calling to a deeper and more substantial life, he felt the need to simplify his material life to accompany his inner simplification. He was compelled to devote himself more completely to his spiritual work.

A major focus in Gandhi's spiritual work was the elimination of violence from his own life. He became more conscious of the subtle forms of violence in his way of relating to his wife. He had felt that it was right to dominate and impose his will on her. She always responded with quiet submission to the suffering he caused her. In the end, it was she who became his teacher in nonviolence. She fully lived the concept of nonviolence in her life.

Gandhi undertook to perfect his relationship with his wife by taking a vow of chastity. Sex for him was little more than satisfying his physical desires and symbolized his attachment to the level of instinct and passion that he yearned to transcend. The transformation of his sexual energies was necessary for a complete and integral commitment to nonviolence.

He worked to unify and harmonize his life. He could no longer live with a gap between what he taught and what he practiced.

Gandhi was very compassionate, always working to alleviate suffering. He took special interest in the well-being of his companions and enjoyed nursing them back to health when they were ill. He was also sensitive to the suffering of animals, and this concern, on one occasion, brought him into conflict with religious doctrine. He had come upon a dying cow that was in great pain. In spite of the Hindu tenet which forbade taking the animal's life under any circumstances, he responded to an inner movement and killed the cow to free it from suffering. He acknowledged a higher truth that transcended dogma.

Gandhi was very free in his approach to life. Much to the frustration of his many political associates, he never worried about being consistent. He frequently changed his mind about issues and approaches, never being afraid of making mistakes or openly admitting his errors in judgment.

He recognized that an individual's concept of truth changes as his consciousness expands. One must always work to learn more about life, to increase knowledge, and to deepen understanding. But expansion of consciousness is more than accumulating information and creating increasingly complex theories. It requires a fundamental change in one's way of living. Gandhi showed us that this transformation must occur at the very roots of our being and include all the elements of our life; the way we think, feel, and act. He knew that the bedrock of a new society was the transformation of each individual.

Another dogma that Gandhi struggled to eliminate was the barrier that stood between the untouchables--the lowest Hindu caste--and all other Hindus. While working in South Africa as a lawyer, representing Indian laborers who were being subjected to racial discrimination, he befriended many untouchables and even took some into his home, even though he was forbidden by Hindu tradition to associate with them. He dedicated much of his later work in India to eliminating the dogmas that separated Hindus from one another and those that separated Hindus from people of other religions, especially the Moslems.

Gandhi never perceived of himself as a guru. Even though he was deeply religious and prayed often, he saw the need to transform and purify himself and humanity in the most practical sense. He offered his life as a symbol of the possibilities that all share.

Gandhi's personal life was integral and harmonious. He often equated his religious life with his political one, recognizing the need to balance action with contemplation. Even during the busiest times and in the midst of strenous negotiations, he took long walks daily and devoted some time each day to manual work. He also dedicated one day each week to being in complete silence.

In 1906, Gandhi embarked on a struggle that was to keep him in South Africa for eight more years and would launch him to the forefronts of Indian politics for the next 40 years. His continuing work of self-transformation was now to receive a test in the political realm as he initiated a campaign of truth and nonviolence.

The government of South Africa had passed a law requiring the registration of nearly all Indians in the country and restricting their travel between provinces. Another part of the law recognized only Christian marriages as valid, nullifying the Hindu and Moslem marriages of the Indians.

Gandhi immediately spoke out against these injustices and proposed that all Indians who were willing and able should refuse to register with the government and openly face the possibility of imprisonment without fear or resentment. During this struggle, hundreds were sent to prison. This was Gandhi's first experiment of nonviolent direct action. His ideas began to take root, and his nonviolent army grew.

Besides refusing to register, many of his followers courted arrest by traveling to other provinces. The campaign expanded when indentured Indian coal miners went on strike at Newcastle. The strike had a serious effect on the South African economy and could have become devastating because the white employees of the nation's railroads also went out on strike. However, at this point, Gandhi called off the miners strike. His reason for doing so was to cultivate trust with his adversaries in the government and to avoid taking advantage of their vulnerable situation. He also wanted to avoid establishing an alliance with the railway workers whose grievances were quite different from those of the Indians.

During the long protest against the policies of South Africa, Gandhi's main adversary in the government was General Smuts. In negotiations with Gandhi, General Smuts often made concessions that he later reversed. These betrayals seriously threatened Gandhi's strength as the leader of the Indians in South Africa and tested his commitment to nonviolent ideas. Many of his followers were losing patience with Gandhi, who insisted on continuing to trust General Smuts, in spite of his broken promises. Gandhi resisted this tide of anger and resentment among his followers to elevate the struggle to a higher level. The purpose of nonviolent resistence was to transcend the "eye for an eye" consciousness, to halt the chain reaction that habitually results from conflict.

Gandhi's perseverence and patience finally paid off in 1914 with the passage of the Indian Relief Bill which reversed nearly all of the Registration Act of 1906. This was a clear victory for Gandhi and his fellow Indians in South Africa, but most importantly, this was a victory for Satyagraha, soul force.

Satyagraha was a vitally important idea that Gandhi gave to the world. He coined the word from satya, or truth implying love, and agraha, or firmness and strength. He called the movement in South Africa Satyagraha because it was a spiritual force born out of truth and love. Gandhi believed that Satyagraha lay latent in all human beings whether they realized it or not. It was the duty of each individual to discover the possibility within himself. Ahimsa, another important word of his, comes from the Sanskrit meaning "without any desire to kill." Ahimsa is the cornerstone of Satyagraha, it is supreme nonviolence. Nonviolence, according to Gandhi, was not passivity or weakness. It was pure inner strength, it was will. And these ideas were to receive the ultimate test upon Gandhi's return to India.

Gandhi returned to India in January, 1915. He was now 45 years old and had spent the last 20 years in South Africa. His reputation as a spiritual and political leader had spread throughout India, where he was now called Mahatma, or great soul. He was to spend the next 31 years in the struggle to liberate India from British rule. In this work, he felt that it was essential for India to be strong and unified in its desire for freedom while being flexible and tolerant of its inherent diversity. Only if the Indians were capable of resolving their divisive conflicts could they be capable of earning and establishing their independence. Using the techniques of civil disobedience and noncooperation, he responded to specific situations where Indian people were being exploited by the British.

Gandhi's first major act of civil disobedience against England was a three-day nationwide strike protesting the continuation of repressive measures imposed by the British during World War I. In spite of the apparent success of this strike, there was enough anti-British violence for Gandhi to be forced to call off the campaign early and to reconsider its effectiveness.

The violence during the strike, however, seemed to pale in comparison with the atrocity committed by the British General Dyer in the city of Amritsar. The General and his army officers fired on an unarmed crowd of between 10,000 and 20,000 Indians attending an unauthorized meeting at Jallianwalla Bagh. Over 1,500 people were killed or injured. The Jallianwalla Bagh massacre horrified Indians and dangerously intensified their hostility towards the British.

This incident marked a turning point in Gandhi's relationship with the British. His respect for their civility was forever marred. Not sacrificing his commitment to nonviolence, he realized that more extreme measures were needed. Thus, he embarked on a policy of complete noncooperation with the British.

Many of those who followed the Mahatma gave up government jobs, stopped attending the universities, and quit the British courts. The emphasis of the policy of noncooperation shifted from the cities to the rural villages. It was in the villages, Gandhi believed, where the real strength of India lay hidden. He envisioned a decentralized economy, with small cottage industries in each village, the industries being run by local villagers and providing for the needs of that community. He recognized the need for simple technology, rejecting the complex technology of the West which he felt degraded people into being slaves to machinery.

One of the cornerstones of Gandhi's policy of noncooperation with the British was the homespun movement. Through the rejection of foreign-made clothing and the reliance of clothing made at home, India expressed its independence in simple but concrete terms. The homespun movement had an impact on the British economy, putting many millworkers back in England out of work. On a trip to England, Gandhi met with these workers, who were understandably hostile at losing their business. Yet, Gandhi described the extreme poverty of India and its urgent need for self-sufficiency. Gandhi's courageous commitment to truth and his humble and friendly demeanor allowed him to win the respect and friendship of these workers. From then on, Gandhi would spend a half hour each day spinning. This simple work with his hands was a prayer.

Gandhi published a weekly magazine titled Young India. His views on noncooperation with the British government were explained in three articles, published between 1921 and 1922. The British viewed his words as seditious and arrested him. He was tried, convicted, and sentenced to six years in prison. Gandhi was released, however, after having spent less than two years in prison, because of an ailment suffered following an appendectomy. He was greatly weakened by this condition but was able to regain his strength in a matter of weeks.

One of India's greatest weaknesses was the hostility between Hindus and Moslems. Gandhi recognized that, until India was purified of this divisiveness, it would never be a free and independent nation. In order to begin to resolve this deeply imbedded conflict, Gandhi undertook a 21-day fast at the home of a Moslem friend and under the care of a Christian missionary. Unfortunately, this fast seemed to have little impact on the friction between Hindus and Moslems in India.

In December, 1929, the Indian Congress adopted a resolution of complete independence from England. Going beyond the struggle for dominion status within

79

the British Empire, this was a call for secession. Gandhi, as the leader closest to the heartbeat of his country, was chosen to lead a new campaign of noncooperation against the British. Since he was worried about civil disobedience getting out of hand and becoming violent, he sought an act of protest that would have a significant effect on the British while unifying his people and elevating their struggle beyond violent means.

Gandhi and 78 companions from his ashram undertook a 24-day, 240-mile march to the sea. This was a well-publicized journey that captured the imagination of India. By the end of the journey, he had thousands marching with him. Upon reaching the ocean, Gandhi picked up a handful of salt left by the waves. By doing so, he openly defied a law that made it illegal to possess salt not purchased from the government. This seemingly insignificant act was the beginning of the end of British rule in India. The country was brought together in a single movement for freedom. The protest against the salt law, which was an obvious injustice against the poor of India, spread throughout the land. The most important aspect of the struggle was that it continued successfully as a nonviolent protest. The nonviolent Indians who suffered the brutality of the British became the moral victors. The supposedly superior Europeans demonstrated their most primitive tendencies to dominate and subjugate those whom they considered their inferiors.

Gandhi, never satisfied with success, continued to struggle to bring his people together in other ways as well. The caste system, which he once defended as providing a place in society and a purpose for each individual, he now rejected and sought to eliminate.

He was especially concerned with the plight of the untouchables who were never allowed to participate in Hindu society.

In order to reduce the violence within and between religions, the British proposed that India be divided into three different electorates: Moslems, Hindus, and Untouchables. Individuals from each group would be elected by, and would represent only, that group. Gandhi was certainly in favor of equal representation but was completely opposed to this method in that it institutionalized their differences and further separated Indians from one another. He was so strongly against this proposal that he undertook a fast that would last until his death unless another way was found. Gandhi's fast went to the heart of India, commanding the undivided attention of all its people. As Gandhi's health subsided, as death neared, India became one nation. Orthodox Hindu temples opened their doors to untouchables for the first time in hundreds of years. Moslems, Hindus, and untouchables came together and worked feverishly to find another way to elect members of Congress which would represent all of India's people. Finally, very near death, Gandhi agreed to a compromise proposal and broke his fast.

In spite of such progress, the hostility between Hindus and Moslems continued to erupt. The fire was fueled by Ali Jimah, a Moslem who led the movement to create an independent Moslem state. Gandhi found this idea repugnant and struggled unceasingly to bring Hindus and Moslems together into one free and independent India.

Gandhi was now 78 years old. He was fasting to reach the souls of all Hindus and Moslems. The split between them was becoming ever greater as the partitioning of Pakistan from India had begun. The violence had reached extreme levels. Gandhi was sickened. He had gone into the war zone courageously risking his life but was unable to stop the tide of religious hate that had been brewing for centuries. On April 30, 1948, while he was arriving at a prayer meeting, Mahatma Gandhi was shot and killed by an assassin.

Mahatma Gandhi indentified with all people because he considered himself imperfect, never superior to anyone else. His life was like an open book, having no secrets or hidden motives. He wanted his life to serve as an example for all humanity, to demonstrate that it is possible for each person to transform himself into a more perfect expression of love, to overcome selfish preoccupations, and to cultivate a life of sacrifice and service.

The effort that Gandhi made in transforming himself led to understandings that he shared with the world. He provided practical tools for liberation. Instead of abstract intellectual concepts that only a few could understand or employ in their own lives, the principles that he worked with were for all people.

He taught by example, his teachings being based on his own work of self-transformation. To Gandhi, self-control was the key to happiness. Only when we are free of the attachments to instincts and passions can we be truly at peace. Violence is to be out of control, and the evil in the world is a reflection of the violence within each of us. We have a dual responsibility, to transform and purify ourselves inwardly as we struggle to overcome suffering and injustice in the world.

The practical aspects of resolving a conflict nonviolently involve the purification of one's intentions. Instead of begin concerned with winning an argument or defeating an opponent, one must undertake a humble search for the broader truth. By cultivating a friendly and trusting relationship, one can become partners with the opponent in understanding and rooting out the deep source of the conflict.

It takes great courage and strength to be nonviolent. One must be flexible and open-minded and capable of re-evaluating and changing one's position when dictated by truth. One must also trust and support the opponent and even suffer for him if necessary. When one fails in efforts to reason, to appeal to the mind, one may use self-suffering as a way of reaching the heart.

In resolving a conflict nonviolently, the means are more important than the ends. If the solution is contaminated with any violence, a seed of resentment will remain to grow into another conflict. Only when the means are pure, will the resolution be permanent. The true test of nonviolence, according to Gandhi, is when no rancor is left behind and when, in the end, all enemies are converted into friends.

Based on the presentation by Gregory Bennett.
Opening quotation from Krishna Kripalan, <u>All Men Are Brothers</u>.

References and Recommended Readings

Easwaran, Eknath. Gandhi: The Man. Petaluma:
    Blue Mountain Center of Meditation, 1972.

Fischer, Louis. The Life of Mahatma Gandhi. New
    York: Harper and Row, 1950.

_____. Gandhi: His Life and Message for the World.
    New York: New American Library, 1954.

Kripalan, Krishna, editor. All Men Are Brothers:
    Life and Thoughts of Mahatma Gandhi as Told in
    His Own Words. The Navajivan Trust, 1960.

Merton, Thomas, editor. Gandhi on Non-Violence.
    New York: New Directions, 1965.

Ramachandran, G., and T. K. Mahadevan. Gandhi:
    His Relevance for our Times. Gandhi Peace
    Foundation, 1967.

MARIA MONTESSORI
Educator

> The child, instead of being a burden,
> shows himself to us as the greatest and
> most consoling of nature's wonders! We
> find ourselves confronted by a being no
> longer thought of as helpless . . . but one
> whose dignity increases in the measure to
> which we see in him the builder of our
> own minds; [he is] the greatest marvel of
> the Universe, the human being.

Maria Montessori made a great contribution to the world in drawing attention to the importance of children as humanity's future. She emphasized the need to understand our way of relating to children and the environments that we provide for them. As a teacher, she articulated the importance of spiritual values for children and of looking at the child as a miracle of creation.

She was able to make many discoveries about children by looking at them with the detached eye of the scientific investigator, but always with the warmth, love, and respect of the ideal mother.

Maria Montessori was born on August 31, 1870, in the province of Ancona in Italy. Her father was employed by the government, and he came from a noble family. Her mother, Renilde Stoppani, was unusually well-educated for a woman of the times. She was described as a lady of piety and charm, and Maria and her mother had profound love and understanding between them.

When Maria was five years old, her parents moved to Rome to be able to provide her with a better education. Maria was extremely interested in mathematics and science which were unusual interests for a girl. The local girls' school did not even offer courses for her to pursue her expanding interest in math and science, consequently, she attended classes at a technical school for boys. At this time she voiced the desire to pursue a career as an engineer, but this was an especially unheard-of career for a woman. Her parents encouraged her to become a teacher because it was generally the only career open to women at that time. But Maria refused to even consider being a teacher. Her interests grew, and she developed an overriding interest in biology, deciding to study medicine. This decision distressed her parents greatly--women simply did not attend medical school.

But, Maria was determined to fulfill her goal, and her determination moved her mother, who eventually became her biggest source of support. At first--not surprisingly--she was refused admittance to the medical school, but after much struggle and, finally, with an appeal to the Pope himself, she was admitted as the first woman medical student in Italy. She won scholarships throughout her years of study and also augmented her income by giving private tutoring. She largely paid her own way through the university.

Maria confronted many difficulties during her student days, primarily from male students who resented her presence in a school that traditionally had been all-male. She was not allowed to dissect dead bodies in the presence of male students as it was considered improper and, thus, had to do her dissecting work in the evenings, alone.

She also had to deal with the overt opposition of her own father to her decision to study medicine. She became discouraged under the oppression of this compounded opposition and at one point reached the decision to drop out of medical school and seek a less-controversial career.

But Maria experienced an unusual occurrence that strengthened her resolve. One day, as she left the school, determined to quit, she came upon a poor woman begging in the streets, accompanied by her two-year-old child who was playing with some colored paper on the ground. Something came over Maria as she looked into the face of this poor child. The child seemed totally unaware of the harsh realities of the life of poverty that surrounded her; she seemed transfixed into an inner state of peace and wonder. This look of inner peace and happiness independent of external circumstances touched and inspired Maria on such a deep level that she turned around and went straight back to the dissecting room. From that moment on she was determined to persevere and continue on with her chosen work. From that moment, too, she never doubted that she had a vocation.

Her life was to demonstrate the principle she was to preach in later years: "The preparations of life are indirect."

During this period of much opposition, she received a great deal of support from her mother. She was a constant friend and sympathizer and always a source of encouragement.

Her father's feelings of opposition to her choice of career changed after he heard her deliver a lecture at the university. She did such a brilliant job in delivering her topic that her father was extremely proud of her.

In 1896 Maria became the first woman in Italy to take the degree of Doctor of Medicine. In that same year she also was chosen to represent the women of Italy at a feminist congress held in Berlin at which she gave a speech supporting the cause of working women. A few years later she attended a similar congress in London where she attacked the practice of exploiting child labor.

In terms of her professional career, after graduation, Dr. Montessori was appointed assistant doctor at the Psychiatric Clinic in the University of Rome. During this period she became interested in mentally retarded children. She came to see that mental deficiency was a pedagogical problem rather than a medical one.

Through her interest in "defective" children, she came in contact with the work and ideas of innovative educators, such as Jean Itard and Eduard Sequin, who devoted their lives to the education of the handicapped. In 1899, at a pedagogical congress, she delivered an address on "Moral Education" in which she advocated that retarded children needed and were entitled to the benefits of education as much as normal children. Because of this lecture, she was asked to give a series of lectures in Rome on the education of the feeble-minded. She compiled a great deal of information on this subject and, when a state orthophrenic school was opened, Dr. Montessori was named the director, a position she held for two years, from 1899 to 1901. She also participated in the actual teaching of these retarded children herself. And through her work with these children, she also became interested in the teaching of normal children also.

After a time, Maria resigned from the orthophrenic school and began to feel the need for further study and meditation. She registered as a student again to study philosophy and psychology. It was an important time of retreat for her, of re-evaluation, and of expanding her knowledge. She returned to her studies with children with new perspectives and insights.

During these years, in addition to her work with retarded children and her general study, she also studied nervous diseases of children and published the results. From 1896 to 1906, she occupied the Chair of Hygiene at the Magistero Femmile in Rome and also was one of the examiners in the Faculty of Pedagogy. In 1904, Dr. Montessori was made a Professor at the University of Rome where for four years she occupied the chair of Anthropology. Her major publication was a large volume entitled Pedagogical Anthropology.

In addition to her work as a lecturer at the University of Rome and the Women's Training College, she also practiced in the clinics and hospitals in Rome and had a private practice. She was extremely concerned about all aspects of her work and further developed her thinking on the philosophy and methods of education.

She also continued to be very interested in the education of normal children, but this field was closed to anyone not part of the state school system. Her chance to work with educating normal children came when she was asked in 1906 to direct a facility that would care for the young children not yet in a state school who lived in a poor area of San Lorenzo.

In her work with these children, she used the materials she had developed in her work with the retarded children. She found that these materials captured the children's attention in a very profound manner. And, thus, she developed more and varied materials, and the overall classroom environment developed further as the focus of her method.

The specific discoveries that she made concerning the nature and education of children are varied. She found that children have an amazing ability for concentration, they learn by and love repetition, they love order, and they learn best when given "free choice of activity." To the amazement of many, she discovered that children preferred work to play, that they had no need for rewards and punishments, and that they actually loved silence. In providing these children with an orderly but free environment, she discovered that they had a spontaneous self-discipline coming from within.

By giving these children a nurturing, free, ordered, and supportive environment, they became eager for learning of all kinds. They learned reading, writing, math, and general life and science principles. The role of the teacher is very different in a Montessori School from traditional schools. The teachers do not tell the children about reality but rather provide the materials for them to learn through their senses.

From her discovery that children love order, she incorporated in her educational method teaching children to clean up after themselves and to always return things to their proper place. She also observed that children love work, that they love to engage in truly constructive activities.

Maria also saw that young children had the ability to engage in what she called "spontaneous concentration." This concentration needs to be respected and not interrupted with activities directed by adults. In her schools she thus advocated that children be allowed to freely work within the environment and that their love of silence and working alone be respected. She also saw that children had the ability to make real choices and to respond with more than curiosity. She also advocated that children should be encouraged to be as independent as possible. She saw that in her schools the normalized children helped each other and were not competitive or jealous.

Dr. Montessori also became aware that young children are truly fascinated with external reality. She felt that fairy tales and other fantasy activities were not necessary for stimulating young children. Reality is itself magical and mystical for them and the external reality imposes the discipline and limits on the intellect that are necessary for healthy development.

She also saw that children who had been "normalized" through relating to the prepared environment were not possessive in their activities. They reached the stage where the knowledge of the object is more important than the object itself. Dr. Montessori once said that members of religious orders and these normalized children seemed to have the same nonpossessive attitude toward property. The idea, "To use and not to possess," guided them.

In the prepared environment, normalized children were very obedient, which springs from "spontaneous self-discipline." This self-discipline takes place naturally within an environment of liberty and respect for the child. Children participating in these prepared environments emulate a sense of joy and happiness.

Maria Montessori's work had such scope and depth because it encompassed all aspects of a child's life. She also discovered certain concepts that are a foundation for her method.

One such concept is that of the child being in stages of metamorphosis. The child's stages of development are distinct one from another. She compared these stages to the metamorphosis of a butterfly. She felt that the child's mind actually functioned differently depending on the stage of development. She also felt that each individual child goes into differing stages at their own different times. In her schools she had materials for these different stages, and children were free to use them whenever the time was right.

She also did work with articulating the importance and character of certain "sensitive periods" that children go through. During these periods they seem to have an ability to simply absorb from the environment whatever is needed. She pointed out sensitive periods for language, order, small objects, refinement of the senses, good manners, and more.

Throughout her time of working with these poor children, she continuously observed children with the love and wonder of a mother but also with the objective eye of a scientist. The work that was done in the name of these children was truly amazing. Word began to spread about the accomplishments of Maria Montessori and these children. People from many countries and positions in life became interested in her approach to educating the young.

Maria began to realize that education was indeed her mission in life. She resigned from her university position and from her practice as a physician and completely dedicated her time and energy to work with children and their education.

Her fame spread, and she was asked to come to speak in various countries. She came to the United States and gave a speech at Carnegie Hall to more than 5,000 people, while many more who wanted to be there were turned away. The welcome from the Americans was enthusiastic. While in the United States she stayed as a guest with Thomas Edison, the famous inventor, who had a great admiration for her work. An American Montessori Society existed under the presidency of Alexander Graham Bell, the inventor of the telephone. The honorary secretary of this society was Miss Margaret Wilson, daughter of the President of the United States. Dr. Montessori gave courses for teachers in California. She also had a Montessori class operating as an exhibition at the San Francisco World Exhibition where it received two gold medals. The prospect of a large Montessori World Headquarters established in America was offered to her, but she felt her ties with Europe too strongly.

She made many trips to all parts of the world to give lectures and set up training courses for teachers. But, she felt her main work was with children directly--to work with them in discovering what was the best method of education. She always had a penetrating insight into the soul of the child. With her scientific outlook, combined with her maternal tenderness and sympathy, she was able to establish a truly respectful and always expanding method of educating children.

In 1939, she was in India giving training courses when World War II broke out. Because she was Italian, she was regarded officially as an enemy alien; however, an exception was made in her case, and she was allowed to continue with her work. During her stay in India, she spent time with Mahatma Gandhi, Mr. Nehru, and Tagore.

In 1946, when the War was over, she returned to Europe and directed an international training course in London. She was asked to return to Italy in 1947 to reestablish the Opera Montessori which had been discontinued during the Fascist regime. And then in 1948, at the age of 78, she returned to India to give more training courses.

The last years of Dr. Montessori's life were full of activity as they had been all her life. Her son, Mario Montessori, helped her by assuming more and more of the responsibility for the directing and coordinating of the work of the Association Montessori International, a position he fully took over after the death of his mother.

Maria Montessori died at the age of 81, on May 6, 1952, in Holland. Her work has influenced our relationship with children throughout the world. Maria Montessori's contribution to humanity has long outlived her own personal life. The spirit of her work is being continued by many souls.

Based on the presentation by Karen Kaho.
Opening quotation from Maria Montessori, <u>The Ab-</u>
<u>sorbent Mind.</u>

References and Recommended Readings:

Montessori, Maria. <u>The Absorbent Mind.</u> New York:
Holt, Rinehart and Wilson, 1967.

_____. <u>The Discovery of the Child.</u> New York:
Ballantine Books, 1972.

_____. <u>Education and Peace.</u> Chicago: Regnery,
1972.

_____. <u>The Secret of Childhood.</u> London:
Longmans, Green and Company, 1936.

Standing, E. M. <u>Maria Montessori: Her Life and</u>
<u>Work.</u> Fresno: Library Guild, 1957.

RAMAKRISHNA
Bridge Between East and West

> *God can be realized through all paths. All religions are true. The important thing is to reach the roof. You can reach it by stone stairs or by wooden stairs or by bamboo steps or by a rope . . . . God is one, but His Names are Many.*

Sri Ramakrishna, a Hindu saint who lived in India during the last half of the 19th century, has been called one of the great religious lights of the modern world. Through the example of his own life and the inspiration of his teachings, many Hindus and non-Hindus alike have found Ramakrishna to be a companion and guide on their own spiritual journey. Neither a great scholar nor a great "doer," Ramakrishna's gifts to humanity are his deep humility and love for the Divine. Within India, the example of this great soul has helped many Indians to understand and appreciate the spiritual depths of Hinduism, and in the West the followers of Ramakrishna have been instrumental in transmitting the insights of Indian spirituality to Western culture.

Born to deeply religious parents in a small village in Bengal in 1836, Ramakrishna's birth was marked by a vision which his father and mother had received nine months earlier. In this vision, the Lord Vishnu--one of the main dieties of the Hindu religion--promised Ramakrishna's father that He would be born to him as a son. Ramakrishna's mother received a similar vision outside the temple of Shiva--another diety of the Hindu religion--which indicated to her the birth of a divine child.

Aside from these remarkable beginnings, Ramakrishna had a simple and joyful childhood. Even at an early age, his intelligence and incredible memory were noticeable. The main characteristic of his personality at this age seemed to have been his overwhelming religious devotion. He was fond of learning the many tales of the Hindu gods and goddesses and loved nothing better than serving the many monks who traveled through his small village.

At the age of 16, Ramakrishna left his native village to go to Calcutta in order to live with an older brother who had established a Sanskrit institute there. This brother tried his best to interest Ramakrishna in all the worldly pleasures and material rewards which would be gained by a scholar in a city like Calcutta, then the most materialistic of India's cities. However, these efforts were in vain, and Ramakrishna showed no interest whatsoever in his studies nor in any material benefits which might result from his studies. His only interest was, as he told his brother, to find God and to live continuously in the presence of God.

A year after his arrival in Calcutta, Ramakrishna's brother accepted a post as a temple priest in a newly constructed temple compound on the banks of the Ganges. He served only briefly in this post, however, dying shortly after beginning his duties. Ramakrishna then decided to take his brother's place as a priest in this temple compound, not knowing that he would spend almost all of the remaining years of his life within its walls. Ramakrishna was asked to serve as priest in the main temple, which was dedicated to Kali, the Divine Mother of the Universe.

As Ramakrishna began to serve in the temple of Kali, he became more and more captivated by Her. Although for many Westerners as well as Hindus the image of Kali is repulsive, symbolizing all the miseries and terror of human existence, Ramakrishna saw only Her maternal, creative aspect, the life-creating force which brings all existence into being. At times the image seemed real to him, it seemed to dance and to speak, and the whole temple was alive with Her presence. Ramakrishna spent his time absorbed in the quest for a direct and continual relationship with the Divine Mother. At times, he was flooded with radiance and joy as he felt Her nearness; at other times, he felt himself to be plunged to the bottom of an abyss where Kali was not and no light could penetrate.

Ramakrishna prayed unceasingly to Kali to grant him a vision of Herself and to reassure him that She was not a figment of his imagination. His tears and prayers were soon answered with one blinding vision of Kali, but this vision only made the priest yearn all the more for a permanent union with the Divine Mother. Gradually, bit by bit, Kali revealed Herself to Ramakrishna until the moment when he was in almost continual awareness of Her presence. She became his guide, and Ramakrishna became Her child.

Ramakrishna's almost continual absorption in the rapture of his relationship with Kali, or his despair

caused by Her absence, greatly affected the perform-
ance of his duties as a priest. He became increasingly distracted in his worship and often failed to carry
out the prescribed rituals, his inner vision directing
him to perform the rites in a manner other than
prescribed by tradition. To others, Ramakrishna's
actions appeared to be those of an insane person, and
Ramakrishna himself often feared for his own sanity.
The woman who had constructed the temple compound, Rani Rasmani, decided that Ramakrishna
would benefit from a visit to his mother in the rural
village where he had grown up and where, it was
hoped, the symptoms of his divine madness would
disappear. His mother was in complete accord with
this plan, for she had heard rumors of her son's
disease and had decided for herself that this madness
would be cured if he were married.

Ramakrishna returned home to his rural village
and, surprisingly enough for a man who distained
sexual desire and material gain, he agreed to be
married. The choice of a bride was, however, very
difficult since Ramakrishna's family was poor and did
not have sufficient funds for the wedding ceremony
and the accompanying gifts. Finally, after many
months of searching, Ramakrishna himself indicated
that his bride would be found in a small neighboring
village. As the bride, Sarada Devi, was only five
years old at the time of the wedding, the marriage
was in reality only a betrothal and the bride remained
with her family for another eight years. At that time
Sarada Devi then journeyed to the temple compound
at Dakshineswar, to be close to Ramakrishna and to
learn from his teaching. She remained as his close
companion until the end of his life and served as a
mother to all of his disciples.

After his marriage and the visit with his mother, Ramakrishna returned to Dakshineswar only to find that his divine madness returned with ever greater intensity. He began spending long periods of time in samadhi, mystical contemplation, and became completely oblivious to the world around him. Birds would perch on his head and peck in his hair for grains of food while snakes would crawl over his body; Ramakrishna and the snakes remaining completely oblivious to one another.

To the intense relief of Ramakrishna, who still feared that he was insane, a Hindu nun arrived at Dakshineswar at this time and immediately recognized Ramakrishna as the person for whom she had been searching. This nun, known as the Bhairavi, had had a vision from the Divine Mother in which she was instructed to search for three spiritual seekers for whom she would serve as a guide and a teacher. She had already found the first two and Ramakrishna was the third.

As soon as the Bhairavi and Ramakrishna began to talk, he earnestly asked her if he was insane. The Bhairavi assured Ramakrishna that he was not ill but only suffering the effects of his intense devotion to the Divine Mother, adding that, "My son, everyone in this world is mad; some are mad for money, some for creature comforts, some for name and fame, and you are mad for God."

Through conversation and close contact with Ramakrishna, the Bhairavi became convinced that he was not simply a highly evolved soul but actually an incarnation of divinity, an avatar. In order to prove her position, she arranged for two famous pundits to come to Dakshineswar in order to have a public debate on this subject. After discussion of

Ramakrishna's experiences, and with many examples drawn from the scriptures to prove her case, the two pundits agreed with the Bhairavi. Ramakrishna's spiritual experiences were the certain signs of the rare manifestation of God in man. Upon hearing this verdict, Ramakrishna only commented, "Well, I am glad to learn that after all it is not a disease."

This nun also initiated Ramakrishna into the practices of two Hindu sects, and he was able to rapidly realize the teaching underlying them. This was the first time that Ramakrishna was following any organized tradition; he had always followed his own inner guidance. These were only the first of many religious practices which Ramakrishna was to embrace--he would later worship as a Moslem, a Christian, and a Buddhist. This diversity of religious experiences led to his teaching that all religious paths and traditions are valid and lead to the realization of the Divine if they are followed with sincerity and perseverance. This teaching is Ramakrishna's greatest contribution to humanity. He himself did not seek to found a new religion, and never did, but instead served to remind the world of the unity of all religious and spiritual quests and of the reality for which they all serve.

Ramakrishna had, throughout his years as a temple priest, worshipped the Divine Mother Kali as a personal god, as a god with form who manifested the power of creation. He was also a devotee of Krishna, and for this devotion, spent long hours dressed in woman's clothing and assuming the attitude of Radha, the lover of Krishna. Thus, his devotion had been dualistic, in the sense that he, the worshipper, was separate and distinct from the Divine, the object of worship. In 1865, however,

101

Ramakrishna was initated into the Vedantic tradition in which there is no distinction between the lover and the beloved, between the worshipper and the worshipped. Ramakrishna became, through this initiation, a sunnasin, a monk who has renounced all ties and privileges of the world. Once again, Ramakrishna was to amaze his teacher by his ability to quickly transcend his own previous belief in Kali and the subject-object relationship upon which his devotion to the Divine Mother had been based. Yet, even though Ramakrishna experienced nirvikalpa samadhi, ecstasy in which there is no distinction between the knower and the known, he himself taught that the non-dualistic path of the Vedanta was too rigid a path for the majority of humanity. He was to demonstrate in his own life that the path of devotion, although initially based on the distinction between the worshipper and the Divine, could also lead to unitive knowledge. Therefore, when later asked by disciples the best means for obtaining a vision of God, Ramakrishna replied, "Cry to Him with a yearning heart, and you will see Him. Men weep a jugful of tears for their wives and children. And for money they shed enough tears to flood a river. But who weeps for God? Seek Him with a loving heart."

By this time a great many people began to visit the temple compound because they had heard of the greatness of this temple priest. Many who came to visit Ramakrishna were householders, married, and already involved in the life of the world. These he called the outer circle, while others, those who were to become the future monks of the Ramakrishna Order, were the inner circle of his disciples. Ramakrishna often surprised and alarmed many members of this inner circle by seeming to recognize them the minute that they entered into his presence. He told many that he had seen them in visions prior to their first visits to the temple.

One of the best known of Ramakrishna's disciples was Vivekananda, who would later come to the United States and Western Europe to found the Vedanta Society. Vivekananda, like many of Ramakrishna's disciples, had been trained in the rationalistic methods of the British schools which had been established throughout India in the 19th century. Thus, at first, he was extremely skeptical of the irrational behavior of Ramakrishna, and only accepted him as his guru after many years of questioning. Like many of those who came to visit Ramakrishna, Vivekanada was initially aghast at Ramakrishna's worship of the image of Kali. To the mind of Vivekananda, as to many others in Indian urban society at that time, image worship was a degenerate aspect of Hinduism which needed to be purged, as many aspects did, such as the caste system and child marriage. However, when asked why he continued to worship the image of Kali as well as the other Hindu dieties, Ramakrishna replied that, even if the image were made of clay, there was the necessity for that type of worship. For many people it was the form of worship which most suited their temperament. "God himself," Ramakrishna explained, "has arranged for many ways of worship to suit the varied temperaments of his worshippers in their different stages of growth."

Vivekananda found other points of disagreement with the teachings of Ramakrishna, and, in particular, he was appalled at the implications of the nondualistic teachings of the Vedanta. One day, after having listened to Ramakrishna speak of these teachings, Vivekananda retired to the veranda to smoke a cigaret with a friend and to complain about this teaching. Laughingly he asked, "Can it be that the water pot is God, that the drinking-vessel is God, that everything we see and all of us are God?" As the two were laughing, Ramakrishna walked up to the veranda and touched Vivekananda, he himself going into samadhi. At the touch of his teacher, Vivekananda would later recount, his mind underwent a complete revolution and he was astonished to realize that there was nothing else in the entire universe but God. In silence Vivekananda returned to his house, where he watched his mother preparing the meal. "I sat down to eat, and I saw that everything--the plate, the food, my mother who was serving it and I myself--everything was God and nothing else but God."

In 1885, Ramakrishna experienced the first symptoms of the sickness which would later bring about his death. He had an inflammation of the throat which later hemorrhaged and became cancerous. Ramakrishna was moved to a house in Calcutta in order to be closer to the doctor, and many disciples at first believed that he would recover. This sickness provoked controversy among the disciples, for some believed that since Ramakrishna was an avatar, he was only acting and not really ill, and would recover shortly. Another fraction, among them Vivekananda, maintained that, avatar or not, Ramakrishna was embodied in a human form and it was this form, the body, which was ill.

Meanwhile, Ramakrishna grew steadily worse, and could only drink a small amount of liquids. He was ordered by his doctors not to speak to anyone, nor to enter into samadhi, as it was believed that this aggrevated the cancer. Nonetheless, Ramakrishna continued to speak to all those who came to seek his guidance and could not prevent himself from entering into samadhi since mystical ecstasy was the essence of his nature. At one point, in spite of his intense pain, Ramakrishna spoke to his disciples, in a whisper, "Do you know what I see at this moment? God has become everything. Men and women are just frameworks covered with skin--it is he who is moving their heads and their limbs . . . . I see that God Himself has become the block and the executioner and the sacrificial victim."

Ramakrishna continued to confound his disciples. At times he appeared to be preoccupied with his pain, both the pain of the cancer and the wasting away of the body because of his inability to swallow. Yet, at other times, he appeared to be only playing, and not really in pain at all. However, in August of 1886, a year after he first became ill, Ramakrishna died.

Shortly after the death of Ramakrishna, the Ramakrishna Order--a monastic order--was established by the members of the inner circle of his disciples, with Vivekananda at its head. The young monks spent long years traveling the length and breadth of India, singly and in pairs. It was during this period, in the first decade after the death of Ramakrishna, that Vivekananada decided to establish the Ramakrishna Mission. The purpose of this Mission, which has been established throughout India, is the education of Indian youths in the traditions of both India and the West, an education which is offered by individuals who have renounced all other ties and vocations other than that of service to humanity. The schools and hospitals, libraries and publishing houses of the mission are established alongside the monasteries of the Ramakrishna Order, so that the monks and nuns alternate between periods of service and periods of silence and contemplation.

When Vivekananda first contemplated the establishment of the Ramakrishna Mission, he was unsure of the source of funding for such an ambitious program. He soon realized, however, that the nations of the West, which were extracting much of the material wealth of India during that period, were themselves in great danger of collapse because of the spiritual poverty of their cultures. Therefore, he reasoned, the nations of the West could benefit greatly from the wisdom of Indian spirituality, while, at the same time, contribute materially to the betterment of the Indian people through support of the Ramakrishna Mission.

In 1893, Vivekananda set out to visit the West, first traveling to the Parliament of Religions being held in Chicago. Vivekananda traveled throughout the United States, often appearing as one exhibit of a traveling circus. Aside from the strangeness of his appearance, Vivekananda's mission was successful in that several centers of the Vedanta Society were established during this visit, and a large collection was taken for the establishment of the Ramakrishna Mission in India.

Today, the Ramakrishna Mission--with its schools, hospitals, printing houses, and libraries--and the Ramakrishna Order are living testimonies to the life and teaching of Ramakrishna. For Ramakrishna, service to humanity was service to God. As he told his disciples, "Do not pity him but serve him, serve him by looking on man as God." This service to humanity is performed by individuals who have already realized their own spiritual identity and, thus, the unity of humankind and the universe. It is, therefore, free of the egotism and selfishness which is so characteristic of human endeavors.

Based on the presentation of Marilyn Skiles.
Opening quotation from Mahendra Nath Gupta (M.), The Gospel of Ramakrishna.

References and Recommended Readings

Isherwood, Christopher. Ramakrishna and His Disciples. New York: Simon and Schuster, 1965.

Lemaitre, Solange. Ramakrishna and the Vitality of Hinduism. Translated by Charles Lam Markmann. New York: Funk and Wagnalls, 1969.

M. The Gospel of Sri Ramakrishna. Translated by Swami Nikhilanda. New York: Ramakrishna-Vivekananda Center, 1942.

Vivekananda, Swami. My Master. Volume IV of Vivekananda's Complete Works. New York: Ramakrishna-Vivekananda Center, 1942.

C. G. JUNG
Modern Man in Search of a Soul

> *Man started from an unconscious state*
> *and has ever striven for greater con-*
> *sciousness. The development of con-*
> *sciousness is the burden, the suffering,*
> *and the blessing of mankind.*

The life of Carl Gustav Jung is a story of self-knowledge. It is an exploration of the inner world of the psyche, a study of the world of dreams, myths, and the unconscious. Jung was a psychiatrist, which means--as he liked to remind his patients and students--"doctor of the soul." As a doctor of the soul living in 20th century Europe, Jung witnessed firsthand the spiritual crisis of modern man, evidenced by the atrocities of the first two world wars and with the threat of nuclear war. His work became a search for an understanding of the human psyche, a search for man's soul, an inner journey with the hope that self-knowledge would lead to reconciliation and peace.

Jung was born on July 26, 1875, in Kesswill, Switzerland, on the shores of Lake Constance. His father was a clergyman and his mother was the daughter of a long-established Basel family. When the boy was four, the family moved back to Basel, and here is where Jung grew up. They lived in a large house on the outskirts of town surrounded by the beauty of the Swiss countryside--trees, fields, mountains, and water. In his autobiography, Memories, Dreams, Reflections, Jung records many memories from his childhood. In his earliest memory he remembers lying in his pram in the shadow of a tree. It was a beautiful warm summer day, and golden sunlight darted through the green leaves. The hood of the pram had been left open, and Jung remembers awakening to the gloriousness of the day and a sense of "indescribable well-being." In remembering this, he wrote: "Everything is wholly wonderful, colorful, and splendid."

Another very early memory is of himself sitting in a high chair, spooning up pieces of bread soaked in warm milk. The milk had a particular pleasant, sweet smell. This, he wrote, was when he first consciously became aware of the sense of smell.

He remembers his aunt carrying him outdoors to watch the sunset over the Alps. "Look," she told him, "Everything is all red." And for the first time, the child Jung consciously saw the Alps.

Jung had a rather lonely childhood, having no brother or sisters until a sister was born when he was nine. He found himself often alone with his imagination. He writes in his memoirs of a companion he had in the garden, a huge stone which he would sit upon. He would have conversations with this stone: "I am sitting on top of this stone, and it is underneath." The stone would reply: "I am lying here on this slope, and he is sitting on top of me." Then: "Am I the one who is sitting on the stone, or am I the stone on which he is sitting?" Jung had a soulmate, so to speak, in this stone, with whom he identified so strongly that he was confused about his own identity. In later life Jung was to look back on this incidence as an illustration of one of his most important theories: the universal symbols of the psyche. Jung discovered that the stone in many ancient cultures and in contemporary African and Australian tribes had always been a symbol of the soul, and thus, even as a child living in Switzerland, this symbol could touch him.

Jung's education began at home. His father, in the tradition of the Church, taught him Latin while his mother read to him of exotic religions from an illustrated children's book. These stories facinated him, especially the pictures of the Hindu gods--Brahma, Vishnu, and Shiva. It was a book he was to return to over and over again, and an interest that he developed in his later studies of comparative religions.

The young Jung was happy to go to school for there he found the companions he had lacked at home. He did remarkably well in the subjects that interested him. As he grew older, he considered many different professions. He wanted to study anthropology and become an archeologist: ancient man fascinated him. Theology, too, interested him, though not in his father's sense. In fact, he often argued with his father about matters of religion. His father, of the Swiss Reform Church, felt that one need not question difficult theological concepts, such as the Trinity, but that all one needed in life was faith. Jung strongly objected to this, feeling that what one needed was knowledge through experience. Jung's father ended up having severe problems with his faith; he suffered from depression and was often hospitalized in later life. He was never able to resolve his relationship to God through faith and died a broken man. Jung and his family suffered greatly from this, and this instilled in Jung the realization that something was missing in modern religions that modern man needed. The search for what the human psyche needs became an important part of Jung's work.

Jung finally decided to specialize in medicine, for his true love was biology and the sciences. As he was preparing for his state examination in medicine, Jung knew that he would have to choose a speciality, but he could not decide what it should be. How he decided, he notes in his autobiography, came to him as a surprise. He was reviewing a large stack of books as he studied, and a textbook on psychiatry was the last one he picked up. He had never been particularly interested in psychology before that and, in fact, had had rather bad experiences in the asylums where his father had gone. The preface of the book described psychosis as "diseases of the personality," and at this definition Jung said his heart began to pound. He knew at that moment that he was to study psychiatry. It was a blend of science (through the study of disease) and spiritual studies (through the study of the personality, the soul). So Jung decided to become a doctor of the soul. It was a time in history when psychiatry was still a new science, largely unexplored, and held, by most professionals in the medical field, in suspicion. His family and friends were disappointed at Jung's choice of speciality--he was a very promising student and would have done well in any field--but Jung went on with his decision, knowing in his heart that psychiatry was his vocation.

His first position was as First Assistant Physician at the Burgholzli Psychiatric Clinic in Zurich. He was 25 years old. Here he completed his doctoral dissertation, "On the Psychology and Pathology of So-Called Occult Phenomena," in which he analyzed the seances of a 14-year-old girl whom he had been studying for two years. It was an important first work, and many themes found in his later work took root here.

It was also at the Zurich clinic where Jung began a new kind of research with the insane. He took mentally ill patients very seriously, and this was a new approach; the mentally ill were often (and still are) dismissed as being simply crazy. What he noticed through long hours of observation was that the "nonsense" they spoke actually made sense on a certain level. It was simply a matter of interpretation. For example, one woman often said: "I am deputy of Socrates," which doesn't immediately mean anything to us, but from knowing the woman's case history, he interpreted her to be saying that she was condemned unjustly, as Socrates was, by her treatment at the hospital. Another patient would say, "I shall make noodles for Naples," and what she was doing was compensating for her feelings of inferiority by declaring a most important work to be done--to make the staple food supply for the Italian city. These were very new observations about how the mind works, and Jung's writings on his word-association experiments began to attract attention.

His early papers came to be read by another innovator in the study of psychology of the day, Sigmund Freud. Upon reading Jung's experiments, Freud invited Jung to Vienna, and at their first meeting they found so much in common that they spoke together nonstop for 14 hours. It was the beginning of a friendship and a professional collaboration. Over the years they shared ideas, traveled together (including a tour of America), wrote, and researched. And Freud so admired his younger friend that he intended to "adopt" him as a son and as entrustee of the Freudian school of ideas. But Jung's interests were taking him in other directions. He was expanding the original interests of his dissertation on the occult and conducting research on psychic phenomenon. Freud could not tolerate this, dismissing so completely the possibility of other faculties of the mind that Jung became amazed at the older man's dogmatism. Freud insisted on one law of psychology, one rule by which psychologists could understand human nature, and that was his theory on sexuality. Jung remembers Freud insisting to him one day that "we must make a dogma of it, an unshakable bulwark." Freud's insistence reminded Jung of his own father's insistence on religious faith, and Jung became aware once again of the intolerance and rigidness that dogmatism can bring.

Jung eventually had to break his collaboration with Freud and found himself on outcast in his field at a time when Freud was infallible in the world of analysis. On the publication of Jung's innovative work, Symbols of Transformation, no support came from his professional field; he was dismissed as being too mystical, out of touch with reality.

The year was 1913. It was a time of great trial for Jung. It became for him a time of retreat. He resigned from his professorship at the University of Zurich to devote more time to his private practice and to an understanding of his own inner journey. This journey revealed itself to him in his dreams.

Even as a small boy, Jung had always been fascinated by his dreams. They seemed to him to be an inner, superior voice speaking to him. But his dreams also could worry him. Sometimes their content was of a strange, frightening nature, and he could not understand their meaning. It was at this time in his life that Jung became overwhelmed by a recurrent dream, an image from the subconscious that was so vivid that it overtook him even in his waking hours as he worked at his desk. He saw a river of blood, a red river so deep that it covered all of Europe. All that could be seen above the river was the top of the highest Alps. This vision horrified Jung, he could not understand its meaning, and he feared for his own sanity. He took refuge among the normalcy of his family, his wife and five children, and he writes that he owes to them the strength to survive this period.

Shortly after this, the meaning of his dream became clear. World War I broke out, and the death of millions in Europe became clearly the river of blood of Jung's dream. He came to understand something profound from this experience, and it led to one of his most important ideas. The subconscious works on more that an individual level; there is a collective level at which it operates. There is a collective unconscious, as Jung calls it, that all human beings share, and that all human beings can affect and influence, or be affected and influenced by. And it was an understanding of this collective unconscious that was vital to an understanding of human nature.

Because he was living in neutral Switzerland during the two world wars, Jung came to believe that it was the duty of the psychologists of his country to conduct an intense study of human beings, to learn more abut the collective unconscious, and to investigate the dark side of the psyche that revealed itself as Nazi Germany.

Many volumes came out of this period of Jung's life (his collected works amounting to more than 80 volumes), and he developed many ideas which have now become familiar terminology. The atrocities of the war led to the concept of the shadow in human nature, the dark, powerful side of our nature that can erupt into a horrible collective force. According to Jung, shadow and light are so evenly distributed in the human soul that our very survival is doubtful. And, for this reason, it becomes vital to recognize our own individual shadows so that we can be disattached from the collective one.

Although he would never underestimate the strength of the shadow, Jung believed that within the human soul there existed the possibility for inner fulfillment, for expansion, and for becoming whole. He called this process of inner unfolding, of becoming a complete individual, individuation. This is a process that occurs in all human beings, whether they are conscious of it or not. But by being conscious of this journey, a human being can unfold his or her possibilities much faster. Every human being has an inner story to live, a myth, and it is the discovery of this myth that is the necessary prerequisite for individuation. It is when human beings are not able to discover their own myth that they suffer from a wide range of mental illnesses. As mentioned earlier, our inner journey is documented and revealed to us by dreams. To be able to interpret dreams, then, becomes vital to individuation. And, interestingly, to be able to interpret myths--the stories that man has

115

told throughout the centuries--also leads to inner understanding.

The way that myths work, Jung discovered, was the way that dreams work in the mind. They share the same symbols, and they have a similar function for the soul. Many motifs are found in myths, and these are universal. All cultures share stories of the hero, for example. From Hercules for the Greeks, to Cuchulain for the Irish, to Paul Bunyan for the early pioneers, and Superman or Luke Skywalker in modern times, all heroes from all cultures share the same qualities: superhuman strength and courage. The hero operates as an archetype, a universal symbol which touches all souls. Myths and the characters within them document an inner process--like the hero who needs superhuman strength to overcome the obstacles and dangers of his life, we all need at times superhuman inner strength and courage to combat our inner battles. A myth is real because it documents a real psychic process.

Dreams, too, are real in the sense that they document a real inner event. Dreams, like myths, are full of archetypes, and through a recognition of them, one can more readily understand inner development. Hero archetypes can be found in dreams, as well as archetypes of the shadow. Since the shadow is the dark side of our nature, our opposite, it often reveals itself as a character in our dreams who is opposite to our real physical appearance; for example, is short if we are tall, has dark hair if we are blond. The characters will cause us conflicts and pain, and we have to call on our inner hero strength to overcome the inner struggle. Another character often found in dreams is that of the anima or the animus, our female side if we are a man, or our masculine side if we are a woman. The anima is the world of emotion and feeling in a man, and if unrecognized by him, can reveal itself in waking life in irrational moods. The animus is the world of the intellect and thoughts in a woman, and if unrecognized by her, can lead to irrational opinions. Jung believed that individuation required the reconciliation of all these parts of the soul.

Jung's research touched on something basic, reached an inner core, in his readers, and he found his ideas becoming more and more accepted, studied, and taught. The C. G. Jung Institute was established in Zurich, with students from around the world who wanted to explore further the ideas of myth, dreams, and the unconscious that Jung was discovering. Jung was invited to a lecture tour of the United States where he was glad to study the archetypes of the Americas, visiting Indian pueblos in the southwest. His later years, between his 60s and his 80s, became his most creative, and more work was written at this age than all his years before. He became internationally known and respected.

On meeting the famous Jung, it seemed that everyone's impression was always the same: never had they met anyone who seemed so whole. Jung led his life as a journey of inner reconciliation, as a method of listening to the inner voice. Jung wrote that our inner voice, the voice of dreams, was no less than the voice of the divine within us. One simply needed to listen. In an interview conducted by the BBC in 1959 when he was 83, Jung was asked if he believed in God. "Believe?" he replied. "Belief has always been a difficult word for me. I don't believe, I know." He died quietly in his sleep on an early spring morning in 1961. His friends and students all commented on the thunderstorm that shook the town at the time of his death and the lightening that struck down the tall poplar tree that grew in front of his house.

Based on the presentation by Patricia K. Colleran. Opening quotation from C. G. Jung, Psychological Reflections: A New Anthology of His Writings, 1905-1961.

References and Recommended Readings

Campbell, Joseph, editor. The Portable Jung. New York: The Viking Press, 1971.

Jung, Carl G. Modern Man in Search of a Soul. New York: Harcourt Brace and Co., 1933.

_____. Psychological Reflections: A New Anthology of His Writings. Edited by Jolande Jacobi. Princeton: Princeton University Press, 1973.

_____. Memories, Dreams, Reflections. New York: Vintage Books, 1963.

Jung, Carl G., M. L. von Franz, Joseph L. Henderson, Jolande Jacobi, and Aniela Jaffe, Man and His Symbols. Garden City, New York: Doubleday and Company, 1964.

DAG HAMMARSKJOLD
Statesman

*Goodness is something so simple: always
to live for others, never to seek one's own
advantage.*

Dag Hammarskjold--Swedish diplomat, United
Nations leader, statesman--was in his lifetime a
well-known and admired public servant. And yet, as
it was discovered after his accidental death in 1961,
he was also a remarkably private man. Throughout
his life he had kept a series of secret diaries which
revealed him to be a man concerned not only with the
outer events of the world around him but with the
inner workings of the spiritual side of human beings.
He was a man of action and a man of contemplation.
And his life was an integral blending of these two
seemingly opposite ways of being.

He was the youngest of four brothers, born on
July 29, 1905. The Hammarskjold family was one of
the oldest families in Sweden. Traditionally, the
family worked in public service, and Dag's father, his
two brothers, and himself all went into some sort of
government work. Dag's father had been a professor
of law and a scholar but, due to financial difficulties,
was forced to go into government work in order to
raise a family. He took this step with great sacrifice

119

and yet perfected his work, eventually becoming Prime Minister of Sweden. His main work was in the area of mediation. Sweden has always been a neutral country and has a tradition of interceding between countries that are in conflict with one another. This time--the turn of the century--was a time of great controversy throughout the world. World War I was approaching, Norway split off from Sweden, and conflict was brewing everywhere. In fact, Dag's father became very unpopular in his country. There was a food shortage in Sweden during the war, and the elder Hammarskjold was blamed for it. He ended up being forced to resign as prime minister and returned to a previous position he had as governor of Uppland at Uppsala.

It is interesting to follow the career of the older Hammarskjold because there is a significant parallel with his life and that of his son. Dag went into public service, reached a high position in Sweden, and went on to become Secretary General of the United Nations. Dag had a great deal of respect for his father; he admired the work that he had done. But this respect was also tempered by a resentment because his father tended to be very hard with his four sons and pushed them into public service. Dag held this resentment in his heart for a long time. Dag's father was rather aloof, and Dag was a very sensitive person. This sensitivity he inherited from his mother, and he retained with her a long and fine friendship throughout his adult years.

Dag did his undergraduate work at the University of Solna and studied literature, philosophy, French, and economics. At this time, he discovered the writing of the Christian mystics from the Middle Ages. He developed a real love for them and later accredited them for his inner development. Dag went on to pursue graduate work in economics and had a difficult time with it because of a conflict he had with one of his professors. The professor would not accept his thesis, and Dag was forced to switch to another department because he found this conflict to be unresolvable in any other way. He was very disappointed and upset about this turn of events, and it caused him a great deal of inner turmoil. He ended up getting a bachelor's degree in law before transferring to another school of economics in Stockholm.

Throughout his graduate career, Dag suffered because he felt that his ideas were not as well accepted as they should have been. He was always exploring new approaches which were not welcome in the traditional academic setting. His academic interest began to shift over from an emphasis in research and economics toward that of government service, where he became most successful. It was also as a student, when he was in his early 20s, that Dag began to develop a real spiritual life. It was an inner search and was completely secret from those around him. He began to write a diary which was published after his death as Markings, a beautiful book on his thoughts and philosophy. In this book he wrote about everything that he thought and felt. It is a wonderful thing to read, full of such honesty. Dag was also influenced by another Swede at this time named Bertil Ekman who had been a student who died at the age of 26. Dag copied something from this young Swede which reflects very well what they both were feeling at the same time: "It is not enough to believe in immortality with mind and heart alone. That belief must be part of the will which may then be wholly directed towards death." He then wrote:

"Death must inspire longings toward life, not away from it." Even at a very young age, Dag did not have a morbid kind of fear of death, but saw it as the great challenge of life. Part of a poem he wrote in Markings illustrates this idea when he writes that "Tomorrow we shall meet, death and I." And death, he says, "shall thrust his sword into one who is wide awake. But in the meantime how grievious the memory of hours frittered away."

Death as a companion, as a reminder of the preciousness of the few hours we have on this earth, was an important concept to Dag. He was a very self-disciplined person, and the social behavior of most of the people he came into contact with bothered him greatly. He felt that too many people frittered hours away talking about things that were not really important. He was very disappointed in people who did not want to talk about anything serious. He has a real love for the inner, spiritual life and was not able to find anyone to share this love. He felt that it was a terrible thing, to waste time. This high standard he maintained throughout his lifetime. It was something that he never talked about publicly, and his view of society and the superficial ways in which people related were not revealed until after his death. Many people criticized him for this because they were offended by what he said. They thought that he was a very hard person. But actually, Dag Hammarskjold simply had a desire for perfection for others and for himself.

Much of his early writing centers on this idea of perfection and his preoccupation with his own imperfections. He tended to be very critical of himself and had high personal expectations. He was a very strong person to be able to look at himself so honestly. It was a sign of real integrity which came out in other aspects of his life, particularly his work in the United Nations.

Dag was very influenced by the writings of Martin Buber. Dag developed a personal friendship with Buber, and they wrote many letters to each other. At the time of Dag's death, he was in the process of translating Buber's book, I and Thou into Swedish.

He was especially interested in Buber's view that in modern society we habitually distrust other people. What he called "existential mistrust" is an ingrained way of relating that is very distant and defensive. Dag agreed with this appoach and recognized it as a real problem. He expanded the notion of Buber's idea--which referred to relationships on a person-to-person level--to that of relationships between countries. He carried this out in his work as a diplomat.

He had a fine career in public service. He worked as a government advisor and for the Bank of Sweden. He was also a part of the group know as the Stockholm School of Economics, an organization of young economists who were developing new ideas. Apparently, Dag Hammarskjold was the first who coined the words "planned economy," an approach which Sweden later adopted.

He was not involved in the political arena very much because he was such a mixture of political ideas. Labels did not seem to fit him. People thought he was conservative and social democratic all in one. But he did reach a high level in government by becoming permanent Secretary of State in the Swedish foreign office.

He was very famous for his ability to work. He was the one who would undertake the most difficult problems and finish them off, finding a solution to improve them. Dag Hammarskjold was also known for his moral stature, sense of justice, integrity, and wholehearted commitment to responsibility, all balanced by friendliness to co-workers. Three words that seemed to sum him up were trust, reliance, and good will. And he was an extremely popular person in his work.

Dag Hammarskjold wrote an essay on "The Public Servant in Society," and in it he outlined his philosophy about his work. He felt that the public servant had to be neutral in his relationships. He should always be committed to his work but not committed to any particular personal view. He felt that it was very important to transcend the desire for personal satisfaction in public work.

He became Secretary General of the United Nations on April 10, 1953. It was a time of great world crisis. The first major problem that Dag Hammarskjold dealt with as a representative of the United Nations was in dealing with the Chinese communists. Several American airmen had been shot down in Korea and were being held prisoner by the Chinese. This was a very delicate situation, and Dag had to gather all his diplomatic skills in resolving this problem. He finally was able to get the Americans released, and this success was to lead to a kind of turning point in the history of the U.N. He helped to transform the U.N. into an agency of action. Rather than remaining in the background, in conversation and exchange of viewpoints, Dag Hammarskjold was fearless in his direct involvement with mediation between countries in conflict.

Dag Hammarskjold was also involved in the Suez Canal crisis of 1956 and in the mediation among Arab states over Lebanon and Palestine in 1958. In 1960, he worked on the conflict in the Congo and this was to be his last work. During this crisis, Dag faced the most difficult of all situations in his diplomatic work. He was asked by the Soviet Union to resign, under the allegation that he always made decisions with a bias against the socialist countries. In a remarkably moving speech before the United Nations on October 3, 1960, Dag Hammarskjold made clear his sense of responsibility to the U.N. He pointed out how historical truth is often established: "Once an allegation has been repeated a few times," he said, "it is no longer an allegation. It is an established fact, even if no evidence has been brought out in order to support it. However, facts are facts, and the true facts are there for whomsoever cares for truth." He refused to resign under the political pressure of a super power such as Russia, saying that it was not the big powers that needed the protection of the U.N. but all the others. In the interest of the small nations he would stay, as long as they wished him to. The members of the U.N. showed their approval by an enthusiastic standing ovation.

During the years he spent in New York, Dag carried out a very active private life. He was interested in art and drama and was outstandingly educated about them. He was personally responsible for reviving interest in Eugene O'Neil's plays in America and Europe during the 1950s, and he arranged the staging of many of them in New York. Eugene O'Neil was apparently very appreciative of this effort. Dag also liked modern art and was extremely knowledgeable about it. He went to the

Museum of Modern Art in New York to acquire some works of art to be displayed at the U.N. The curator did not know who he was and thought that he might be the curator of the Royal Swedish Museum because he was so knowledgeable. He was also a collector of books and had a huge, finely bound personal library. He also did translations, making many French and English writers available in Swedish to his native colleagues. He translated the work of a French poet named Persee, and because of its availability to Swedish readers, it won a Nobel Prize. Dag carried on translations even during the most difficult crises. It was a kind of release for him.

Dag Hammarskjold's death in 1961 took place under rather mysterious circumstances. He died in a plane crash in the Congo, and controversy surrounds exactly what happened. Some people thought he was shot down, others thought that maybe he arranged the accident himself. This rather bizarre idea is indicative of the reaction to his book published after his death. People were very critical of him for his private religious feelings. Especially in Scandanavian countries, the spiritual life is something that is not discussed. But some readers recognized the true spiritual search that was part of Hammarskjold's writings. His journals have become a source of inspiriation for those with a similar inner quest.

Based on the presentation by Gregory Bennett.
Opening quotation from Dag Hammarskjold, <u>Markings</u>.

References and Recommended Readings

Hammarskjold, Dag. Markings. New York: Alfred
A. Knopf, 1964.

Stolpe, Sven. Dag Hammarskjold: A Spiritual
Portrait. New York: Charles Scribner's Sons,
1966.

SIMONE WEIL
Modern Saint

> *There is a reality outside the world, that is to say, outside of space and time, outside man's mental universe, outside any sphere whatsoever that is accessible to human faculties. Corresponding to this reality, at the center of the human heart, is the longing for an absolute good, a longing which is always there and is never appeased by any object in this world.*

Simone Weil was born in Paris in 1909 and died in London in 1943 at the age of 34. During her brief life she had been a professor of philosophy, a factory worker, a trade-union militant, a pacifist, a combatant in the Spanish Civil War, an agricultural laborer, and a refugee from war-torn France. She was also a mystical thinker who believed that participation in the suffering and affliction of humanity was the means by which the soul would come in contact with the divine. Her life, both in its exterior and interior aspects, is an inspiration for all those who would follow that ideal.

In her book of essays, Waiting for God, Simone Weil recounts her first awareness, at the age of 14, of her intense longing for "access to that transcendent realm where only the truly great can enter and where truth dwells." Overawed by the intelligence of her brother, she felt herself incapable of entering this realm of truth and fell into a long period of despair. But, after months of inner darkness, she writes that she gained, suddenly and forever, the certainty that any human being who longs to enter into contact with the realm of truth--that realm usually reserved for genius--can do so, if his or her desire is of enough intensity and strength.

Despite the period of despair because of the mediocrity of her natural faculties during her adolescence, Simone was in actual fact a great intellectual. She particularly excelled at mathematics and philosophy, graduating near the top of her class in the Ecole Normale, and the essays which she published on social criticism remain remarkably contemporary. As a student at the university, she was noted not only for her intellectual brilliance but also for her high degree of involvement in the movement for the unification of the French trade unions, in the pacifist movement, and as a teacher at a school for workers. Her lack of attention to dress and her stern individuality also attracted a certain amount of criticism, particularly from the school administrators, many of whom felt a sense of relief when she graduated from the university. Even at this early stage of her life, she turned away from the advantages that she could have had as a brilliant student in order to participate in the larger realm of life.

On her first teaching job, in a small provincial town far from Paris, Simone Weil taught philosophy full time while continuing to work actively with the trade-union movement as well as teach in another school for workers. In addition, she became involved with an organization of unemployed workers in the small town where she lived and led several delegations of these workers on marches to the offices of the city administrators. Not surprisingly, the official reaction to her participation in these marches was unfavorable, and she was transferred to another town at the end of the school year. During this first year of teaching, Simone began the practice of giving away the largest portion of her salary and retaining only a small amount for herself, a practice which she continued throughout all of her life.

During the summer vacation of that year, 1932, Simone spent several months in Germany, studying the effects of the rise to power of Hitler. She returned to France fully convinced of the strength of the Nazi movement and of the danger which it posed for the German working class. She also returned fully disillusioned with the Communist Party, which in her opinion had simply abandoned the German workers to the Nazis as a maneuver of Soviet foreign policy. This experience confirmed her growing conviction that a political transformation of society, one of either the right-wing or the left-wing, would result simply in a different type of oppression for the working class and would not end that oppression.

Simone continued to teach for several years more, after which she requested a leave of absence for, she said, the purpose of writing a thesis on technology and the working class. In actual fact, she had been able to get a job as an unskilled laborer in an electronics factory, and she intended to devote her time to working full-time at the factory. The year which Simone spent working in various factories in Paris was an extremely important period of her life as it marked in many ways a turning point between her concern with purely social problems--which had occupied the first portion of her life--to a concern with social problems set within the framework of a larger reality, that of the divine.

In Waiting for God, Simone describes the effect that the year of factory work had on her, not so much through suffering that she endured but rather through participation in the affliction of all those she saw around her. Her first-hand experience with suffering helped her to understand the suffering of all the world. From that period onward, Simone remarked, she always regarded herself as a slave, and, as such, she discovered a short time later her affinity to Christianity, the religion of slaves. This discovery was the spark from which all her later mystical inspiration flowed.

After being laid off in the factory, her parents took her on a vacation to Portugal during the summer months. There, all alone in a small village, she watched a religious procession of the wives of the fishermen, making a tour of all the ships, carrying candles and singing ancient hymns. She had never heard anything so poignant.

Although Simone Weil had never been antireligious in her life, she had never been religious either. This experience in Portugal was the first intimation of the spiritual yearning within her, a development which she herself had neither forseen nor expected.

In the summer of the following year, 1936, Simone traveled to Spain only a few months after the outbreak of civil war, determined to enlist on the Republican side, even though she remained a pacifist. She found herself on the front lines in a Republican unit in Aragon, which was composed partially of foreigners and partially of Spaniards. Simone spent only a month at the front and was forced to leave for medical care following a cooking accident in which she burned her leg. She left Spain greatly disillusioned with the Republican side, as she had found that in actual practice the relations between the Republican soldiers and the inhabitants of the region, largely peasants, were exactly the same as those between the rich and poor everywhere.

After her return to France, Simone took an extended trip to Italy in order to recuperate from her burn. She found herself enchanted by the Italian cities, particularly Rome and Florence, and spent a great deal of time in meditation in various chapels. She was deeply touched by the life of St. Francis, and she journeyed to the region of Assisi where, she wrote in the little 12th century Romanesque chapel of Santa Maria degli Angeli, a beautiful place where St. Francis often used to pray, something stronger than she was compelled her, for the first time in her life, to fall to her knees in prayer.

After this holiday she returned to teaching, for only a brief period as the intense headaches which had plagued her all of her adult life forced her to take another leave of absence. These headaches, the pain from which was so intense that she could only lie in a darkened room with pillows over her head, were her first and ever present contact with physical affliction and the effects of such affliction on the soul.

During the Easter holiday, in 1938, Simone went for a ten-day stay to the Benedictine Abbey of Solesmes, which is famous for its Gregorian chants. Here, as she explains, she was suffering from severe headaches, so severe that every sound hit her like a blow. This caused her to question the nature of human suffering and the possibility of discovering in the midst of affliction divine love. While at Solesmes, Simone made the acquaintence of a young English Catholic who introduced her to the work of the metaphysical English poets of the 17th century, and, in particular, to George Herbert. She learned the poem "Love," by George Herbert, by heart and would recite this poem to herself as a means of detaching herself from the violent pain of her headaches. In the midst of one of these headaches, the recitation of the poem had the effect of a prayer and, as she later recounted, "Christ himself came down and took possession of me." She felt his personal presence, very real, resembling love.

The mystical revelation which Simone Weil experienced was, while acceptable to her emotionally, was not acceptable to her intellectually. While she was prepared to accept the existence of another reality, that is of God, she was not prepared to accept the possibility of contact between human beings and the divine.

Only after this experience did she begin to study the lives of the mystics as well as to immerse herself in a study of all religions. Through this study not only her love of the divine was deepened, but also her intellectual questions were answered. In this quest to discover the similarity of all the great spiritual traditions, and in answer to her doubts, Simone was greatly aided by the help of two Catholics--one, a priest, and one, a farmer, whom she met a short time later.

Simone Weil was not fated to develop her mysticism during a period of calm and recollection, but rather during a period of brutality and extreme suffering on a massive scale. In 1940, the German

133

army invaded Paris, and Simone and her parents fled to the south of France, eventually settling in Marseilles. Here she wrote and published a number of essays on social and religious themes, many of which have been reproduced in the book, Waiting for God. A central theme in these essays is the misery and affliction of humanity and the deep abyss which separates humanity from the perfection of God. Simone believed that there were two ways by which the soul journeyed toward the divine: one was that of extreme joy, the other was that of affliction. It seemed to her that the latter was the road of humanity.

Affliction for Simone Weil meant a violent uprooting of life, which is manifested to the victim not only through physical and psychological pain, but also through social humiliation. For those who are not at present in affliction, it is difficult and painful to contemplate the pain and suffering of others, for to do so is to contemplate the thin line which separates the one from the other. This result of affliction, if the soul is oriented toward the other reality, is the destruction of the personality, the decreation of the personal 'I', the part of us, wrote Simone, which belongs to error and sin. Through this decreation of the personality, the impersonal can be reached. Thus, affliction, which is the state of extreme and total humiliation, is also the condition for passing over into truth. This condition for passing over into truth is based on the recognition of the limited and finite nature of human existence.

Through the act of accepting suffering, which is the means whereby the soul becomes detached from the self, man accepts the gift of grace. Grace is like a seed implanted by God in the heart of all human beings; like all seeds the development of the seed of grace depends upon the conditions of the garden. It is the orientation of the soul toward God which allows the seed to flower.

Simone benefitted greatly during her stay in Marseilles from conversations with a Catholic priest, Father Perrin, who was the first person with whom Simone discussed her mystical experiences. Father Perrin never tired of urging Simone to become a member of the Catholic Church. Although she was greatly attracted by the spiritual tradition of the Church, she would not join because by doctrine the Church excluded from salvation all those who had not been baptised. Through this good priest, to whom Simone was deeply attached, she met another Catholic philosopher, Gustave Thibbon. As she was not able to teach due to the anti-semitic laws of the Vichy government, Simone had begun seeking work as an agricultural laborer, and in this capacity she was invited to live and work on Thibbon's farm. She found the conditions in the main farmhouse far too comfortable for her taste and soon moved out, into a smaller, ramshackle building some distance from the main house. Some time later she left to become a migrant agricultural worker in the vineyards of the surrounding region.

Before her flight from Paris, Simone had submitted to the French government a plan for a group of front-line nurses who would attend the dead and dying on the field of battle. She considered this as more or less a suicide squad, as the nurses would be under constant fire, but argued that it would have tremendous effect on the morale of the troops as well as saving lives. If the plan were accepted she would have been the first person to volunteer.

Simone felt that she could only adequately argue in favor of this plan if she could present it in person to the Free French government in exile in London. In addition, she wished to get her parents out of France, and they would not leave without her. Consequently, she and her parents set sail on May 17, 1942, for Morocco, and from there to the United States.

From New York, Simone went on alone to London, where she was to work for the Free French government, all the while urging the adoption of the plan for frontline nurses. When it became apparent to her that this plan would not be accepted, she proposed that she be parachuted into France on a mission for the Resistence movement. Her constant requests for a mission were turned down, both because of her obviously Jewish appearance, which would have marked her from the beginning, and because of her physical weakness.

Ever since the German invasion of France, Simone had been eating only the amount of rations given to civilians in occupied France. This factor, combined with her general state of exhaustion and frustration at not being able to join the Resistence within France, all contributed to the contraction of pulmonary tuberculosis, from which she died in 1943. The doctors had originally believed that she could be cured, but because she refused to increase her intake of food, they gave up in despair. Thus, the official cause of death was listed as suicide by starvation, "while the balance of the mind was disturbed."

Simone Weil had not thought for the glorification of herself. Her sole thought and desire was to lose herself in the reality of the work, and through the pain and affliction of that reality, to find her way to God. Her life and her writings stand as a monument to that effort and serve as a guidepost and an inspiration to all those who would follow her.

Written in Italian on a small plaque attached to Simone Weil's gravestone is the following inscription:

> My solitude held in its grasp
> the grief of others till my death.

Based on the presentation by Marilyn Skiles.
Opening quotation from Simone Weil, Waiting for God.

References and Recommended Readings

Weil, Simone, The Need for Roots. New York: Harper and Row Publishers, 1971.

_____. The Notebooks of Simone Weil. London: Routledge and K. Paul, 1976.

_____. The Simone Weil Reader. Edited by George A. Panichas. New York: David McKay Company, Inc., 1977.

_____. Selected Essays, 1934-1943. Edited by Richard Rees. London: Oxford University Press, 1973.

_____. Waiting for God. New York: Capricorn Books, 1959.

W. B. YEATS
Irish Poet and Mystic

> *When a man writes any work of genius, or invents some creative action, is it not because some knowledge or power has come into his mind from beyond his mind? It is called up by an image . . . but our images cannot be given to us, we cannot choose them deliberately.*

William Butler Yeats was many things throughout his pilgrimage of life--he was a poet, a philosopher, a politician, and a playwright. Although he is most famous for his poetry--being called by modern critics the greatest poet in English of this century--it is his life as a pilgrim that holds the greatest teaching. His pilgrimage in life was an inner journey, a search for meaning, for religion. It is a road that began when he was a very small boy roaming the hills of Ireland and carried him through to white-haired old age.

Yeats was born on June 13, 1865 in a suburb of Dublin, Ireland. His father was John Butler Yeats and was, at the time of his oldest son's birth, a promising young lawyer just out of Trinity College. Yeat's mother was Susan Pollexfen, from an old, well-established family in the west of Ireland, and her country relatives were to have a strong influence on Yeats as he grew up. When William was three, his father decided to leave the practice of law and become an artist--a painter--much to the distress of his wife and in-laws. He moved the family to London where there were more opportunities for him to study and to exhibit his art. Fortunately, he was very talented, and he eventually became very successful as a portrait painter. But the early years were rough financially for the family--two sisters and two brothers were born--and to help deal with the problem of supporting her family, Yeat's mother took the children to her family's home in County Sligo, in the northwest of Ireland, for the summer months of every year.

Yeats loved this country--a land of mountains and lakes and changing skies. It was always hard for the Yeats children to go back to the city life of London. Yeats writes in his autobiography a memory of his sister and himself standing in a park in London, holding a lump of earth in each hand, wishing it were soil from Sligo. This is how close they felt to the land there. Both Yeats' mother and father were from Irish Protestant familes, in fact, he had uncles and a great-grandfather who were clergy in the Irish Anglican Church. Yeats went to church with his mother, but admits that the only reason he went was because it was preferable to staying home with his father, who would insist on giving him a history lesson and who, because of a bad temper, often threw books at his son's head. Yeats' father had become very antireligious during his college days at Trinity, becoming a follower of rationalist philosophy and the utilitarian ideas of John Stuart Mill. To Yeats' father, what could not be seen could not be proved.

In that way, it seems very appropriate that he chose as his art form portrait painting, because to him, what was apparent was what was real.

So William grew up without really identifying with being a Protestant, in a country that usually draws a marked distinction between religions. Yet, even as a child, Yeats had a very religious sensibility, and his father's lack of belief bothered him. He wrote in his autobiography:

> "My father's unbelief had set me thinking about the evidences of religion, and I weighed the matter perpetually with great anxiety, for I did not think I could live without religion."

There were many things in Yeats' daily life in the Irish countryside that led him to believe that there were evidences of religion, and these evidences came from what he called the "unseen world." The Irish are very famous for their stories of this world, stories of the invisible; tales of ghosts and apparitions, fairies and leprechauns abound. These are the stories that Yeats grew up on, and he loved them. His grandfather Pollexfen was especially good at telling stories, and many of his relatives and the other towns people would tell of visions they would have or other strange happenings. An aunt of his had the gift of second sight. And, one night, his mother and a servant heard the banshee crying. A banshee is a type of female fairy that many Irish and Scots believe dwells near a particular house, and they are known to foretell a death in the family. The night after his mother had heard the banshee crying, Yeats' youngest brother, Robert, died.

There was also something about the mystery of life that awakened in Yeats a religious love. He used to wander through the hills looking at the sky and the clouds, imagining that God was among them. One night there was a commotion around the household because a cow in the fields was about to calve, and the little William stayed awake as long as he could. By morning, there was a newborn calf and William asked everyong how the calf had gotten there. No one would tell him so he assumed that no one knew. Only one thing was certain: the calf was a gift of God, just as babies were. So he decided that just as soon as he was old enough, he would stay up all night and watch a new calf or baby arrive, to see how it was done. He imagined that God would open up from the clouds in the sky and present the newborn. Then he would know God. He confided this plan to an older boy who was visiting, and this boy--well-informed as he was--promptly explained to little William the facts of life. In remembering this event, Yeats writes in his memoirs that he thereafter was miserable for weeks.

As a teenager, Yeats developed a great desire to be alone. He read Thoreau and wanted to live in imitation of his life. His poem, "The Lake Isle of Innisfree" comes from some of these early ideas that he developed. On warm summer nights he would sneak out of the house to climb a hill and find a cave and wait for the sun to rise. He developed a "passion for the dawn," a theme appearing in many of his poems. The dawn came to mean to him a pure subjectivity of being--a state of peace, free from desires. While other boys his age were learning to love the pleasures of the pub, Yeats longed to live alone, seeking wisdom.

141

As a teenager also, Yeats began to write his first poetry, a practice greatly encouraged by his father. On train rides and trips they discussed all forms of art, talking more about style than content. Writing poetry was sometimes a source of embarrassment for Yeats. He would get so absorbed in what he was writing that he would act out loud in his room the lines or the character he was developing. So the family was often disturbed by the sound of William in his room shouting out a battlescene based on some Irish myth.

Many of Yeats' early poems and plays were based on Irish legends and myths, collected from his relatives and the people of Sligo. When in London, as a student, Yeats was again attracted by tales and stories from the unseen world. He began to go to seances and study the occult sciences. He writes all about the many strange events that would happen at these seances: tables rising, voices coming from no where, strange lights. It goes without saying that his rational father greatly disapproved of these pursuits. But Yeats found among the others interested in these sorts of studies a common bond--people who believed in the possibility of a world beyond this one.

His explorations brought him in contact with one of the most colorful characters of the turn of the century, Madame H. P. Blavatsky. Madame Blavatsky was founder of the Theosophical Society, a society interested in the exploration of the unseen world. Theosophy means divine wisdom, or the accumulated wisdom of the ages. It was founded in 1875 to form the Universal Brotherhood of Humanity, without distinction of race, creed, sex, caste, or color; to encourage the study of Comparative

Religion, Philosophy, and Science; and to investigate
unexplained laws of nature.

Yeats thoughts that here he had found a method,
a means, by which to fulfill his religious quest. His
autobiography is full of stories of his visits with
Madame Blavatsky, full of fascinating dialogue. She
would often sit at her table surrounded by followers,
doodling symbols on a piece of green baise. She was
always surrounded by a crowd, whom she would often
invite to stay for a vegetarian meal. When Yeats
first met Madame Blavatsky, she reminded him of a
kindly Irish peasant woman, and she was full of warm
humor while carrying a sense of audacious power.
She had extraordinary psychic powers, had studied in
India, and had a great deal to teach the young Yeats.
Yeats had a hope about Madame Blavatsky, writing:
"Certainly if wisdom existed anywhere it must be in
some lonely mind admitting no duty to us, communing
with God only." But his relationship with the Theosophists did not last long. Yeats had very definite ideas
about how he wanted to conduct psychic research,
and the Theosophists had theirs, and they eventually
asked Yeats to leave the group because of his insistence on performing certain experiments.

Yeats did find the method that he was seeking,
however, in a secret society known as the Society of
the Golden Dawn. He became an important member
of this society for more than 25 years. It was
founded by McGregor Mathers, a Cabbalist. For
many years, the work of this society was kept secret,
and it was difficult for outsiders to know what kind
of work was done. However, the society (many years
after Yeats had joined) disintegrated from internal
conflicts, and one member published the society's
notes and writings. So now we know that they did

work with the Cabbala, a system of symbols from Jewish mysticism which is used to explain the scriptures and the nature of the universe. They also did work with the Tarot. These pursuits marked the early stages of Yeats' preoccupation with mysticism, and these ideas were to evolve rather dramatically throughout his long life.

Yeats was only 25 years old when he joined the Golden Dawn, and his ideas about mysticism were just beginning to evolve. In his earlier years, he called his preoccupation with mysticism the study of magic. From an essay entitled "Magic" he writes that he believed in the practice and philosophy of what has been throughout the centuries called magic or what he called the invocation of spirits. He believed that the borders of the mind are infinite and that many minds can flow together to create or reveal a single mind, a single energy. Likewise, our memories are always changing and are a part of one great memeory, the memory of nature herself. And, Yeats believed, this great mind and great memory can be evoked by symbols. Yeats writes that he believed that many of the problems of the modern world come from a perishing of the quality of mind that once made these beliefs common over the world.

No essay on the life of Yeats would be complete without the mention of another very important woman that Yeats met in his youth. Her name was Maud Gonne, and she was a famous--or notorious, depending on your view--orator, organizer and revolutionist in the fight for Irish independence that was such a concern at the turn of the century. She had great oratory skills, traveling throughout Europe to plead the cause for the plight of the poor and homeless in Ireland. Ireland had the worst poverty to be found in Europe, and Maud Gonne had a great love and sensitivity for her people. Yeats fell in love with her, and many times for more than 30 years he asked her to marry him. She refused every time, claiming always to be married to politics.

Partly due to his feelings for Maud Gonne, and partly for his feelings for the art of William Morris, Yeats began to attend the meetings of the Socialists. But, no matter how hard he tried, he could not tolerate Karl Marx because of his ideas on religion. This led to arguments at all the meetings, with Yeats storming out one night. He writes in his autobiography: "They attacked religion, (but didn't they know) there must be a change of heart and only religion could make it. What was the use of talking about some new revolution putting all things right, when the change must come, if come it did, with astronomical slowness, like the cooling of the sun, or like the drying of the moon?" This is the idea that guided much of Yeats' reaction to the politics of the next 25 years.

Yeats' adult years saw many changes in the politics of Ireland, with the 1916 revolution, the ensuing years of civil war and, finally, the declaration of the Irish Free State in 1921. Yeats was in and out of politics during these years, sometimes finding himself in a march with Maud Gonne, and later serving as a senator in the new Irish government. But, for the most part, Yeats was distrustful of politics, and many of his poems deal with what can happen to people who become fanatic about a cause.

Yet, Yeats believed very strongly in the cause of Irish independence, though he felt that it must come more from a change of the heart than from a change in legislature. This change of heart took its form for him in art, and it is sometimes said that under Yeats there was an Irish Renaissance in literature. Yeats, along with other playwrights and poets, founded the Irish Dramatic Movement and the Irish Theater. He wrote many plays based on the wealth of Irish myth. He personified Ireland as a woman in his series of plays on the Countess Cathleen and in many poems. In 1923, Yeats received the Nobel Peace Prize for literature, which came to him as a surprise, and by which he was very honored at the international recognition.

Yeats finally did marry, but not until his fifties, and only after asking Maud Gonne one last time to marry him. He married an English woman named Georgiana Hyde-Lees, a friend for many years and whom, he described later, as being the most perfect of companions. His marriage to her ended up shaping his destiny more than he ever could have imagined, because, shortly after his marriage, a series of extraordinary events took place. His wife discovered that she had the gift of automatic writing. She would go into a trance, apparently beyond her control, and write, in a handwriting not her own, about knowledge that she could not know by ordinary means. This took place at intervals for more than seven years, and over this time, information from some superior mind was relayed to Yeats. He writes about these happenings in his formidable prose work, A Vision. One of the things he learned about was the impending crisis of western civilization--he was receiving this information in the 1920s--and Yeats documents this information in what amounts to a geometry of the history of western civilization. He explains that civilization evolves in cycles of 2,000 years--as the Roman and Greek civilizations lasted, and as our Christian civilization has. Since they last only 2,000 years, we are nearing the end of an era. In this system, it is explained that each new civilization begins a kind of reversal of the old: what was once sacred and holy becomes secular, as the Roman gods, once holy, became part of secular myth. Likewise, our civilization will see a great change, and the period of change is always accompanied by a period of chaos, with unavoidable war, totalitarian governments, and repression of freedom. But, in Yeats' system, chaos will evolve into a world with a new religion, new values, and a new, great renaissance in human learning, the arts, and sciences. His system also explains personal history, with personal destines being influenced by the elements of the earth and fire, the sun, and the moon. He fits many famous persons from history into this framework. Yeats considered A Vision to be the most important of his works, and his later poems come from themes found here.

Work on A Vision inspired in Yeats a passion for knowledge that he had not known since boyhood. He read voraciously in philosophy and in Christian and Eastern mysticism in order to understand better this knowledge that had been given to him. He found the most satisfaction for his thirst for knowledge in his readings on the Indian mystics, writing that in Eastern philosophy was found something ancestral to ourselves and which we needed to rediscover in order to appease our Western religious instincts.

Yeats befriended an Indian monk, Shree Purohit Swami, and together they wrote a beautiful translation of the Upanishads, the central wisdom of Hindu thought. Through his friend, Yeats came to understand that mysticism was not so much based on the ability to use psychic powers, as he thought in his early work in magic, but that mysticism was acquiring a state of mind. He wrote that he came to understand that we may never know the truth, but that we can embody it. He wrote numerous essays on Hindu practices of life and prayer, finding there important ideas for Western minds.

Yeats was living in the south of France in January, 1939, recovering in the warmer climate from a series of long illnesses, when he died. He was 74 years old. His body was taken back to the land that he loved, and he was buried in Sligo. He had written his own epitaph, and his tombstone reads:

> Cast a cold eye
> On life, on death
> Horseman, pass by!

Based on the presentation by Patricia K. Colleran. Opening quotation from "Hodos Chameliontos," The Autobiography of William Butler Yeats.

References and Recommended Readings

Blavatsky, H.P. The Secret Doctrine. London: The Theosophical Publishing House, 1968.

Yeats, William Butler. The Autobiography of William Butler Yeats. New York: Collier Books, 1974.

_____. The Collected Poems. New York: Macmillan, 1976.

_____. Essays and Introductions. New York: Collier Books, 1968.

_____. The Ten Principal Upanishads. Put into English by W. B. Yeats and Shree Purohit Swami. London: Faber and Faber, 1975.

_____. A Vision. London: Macmillan and Company, 1937.

E. F. SCHUMACHER
The Economics of Voluntary Simplicity

*The art of living is always to make
a good thing out of a bad thing.*

E. F. Schumacher was an economist by profession, and the title of his famous book, Small Is Beautiful, has become a common expression and idea in our times. Its subtitle, Economics As If People Mattered, illustrates his basic philosophy. He expanded our understanding of the cultural and social consequences of the prevailing style of economic growth, and he demonstrated the possibility of a new approach to development, one in which people--and not just ideas or goals--were taken into consideration. He was an individual committed to life by vocation, and he effectively worked for the welfare of poor communities of the Third World, writing and lecturing with passion to audiences of the industrial nations. He always urged his listeners to work for a more sensible and humane economy. And his ideas became popular because of his integral, holistic approach to solving economic problems.

Ernest Fritz Schumacher was born in Bonn, Germany, in 1911. From his book, A Guide for the Perplexed, one can see that from a very early age he was concerned with the question of the meaning of life. When he was a youth, one of the prevailing modes of thought was that of Positivism. But Schumacher felt that this modern material approach left all questions that really mattered unanswered and that even the validity of such questions was denied. He was searching for more expansive viewpoints and explored alternative approaches to living, such as organic farming, natural foods, healing, and caring for nature, which was consistent with the tradition of naturalism that was well grounded in German nations. His substantivist rather than formalist view of economics is consistent with the German Historical School of Economics. And his integral view of life and his commitment to help mankind are consistent with the teachings of the Perennial Philosophy.

During the 1930s, he studied economics at Columbia University in New York and became a Rhodes Scholar at Oxford University. When the Nazi regime was established in Germany, he emigrated permanently to England in 1937 and made this country his home base for the rest of his life. When World War II broke out, he was interned on a work farm with other German refugees. After a brief internment, he continued to work as a farm laborer until 1943. As a result of this unexpected experience, he developed a sense of reverence for land and learned more about organic farming. He transformed otherwise adverse circumstances into an opportunity to learn. This way of relating to existence was to pervade his future work.

After the war was over, the youthful period of search, formation, and retreat was almost completed, and Schumacher began the creative period of his life, both as a person and as a professional economist.

From 1945 to 1950, he worked as an economic advisor for the British Control Commission in Germany and then spent 20 years as economic advisor to the National Coal Board in London. Through this job, he became very knowledgeable of the political economy of energy sources such as coal and oil. He was a persistent--and, in official eyes, often highly unpopular--one-man early warning system on the dangers of over-dependence on oil and the even greater dangers of nuclear power. In the meantime, he became interested in the process of economic development of the Third World countries.

Some time in the 1950s, he went to Burma to work as an economic advisor to its government. Thus, he began his own "journey to the East." In Burma, Schumacher became aware of the eventual disturbing consequences which the adoption of a Western style of growth will produce in the values and social relations of a traditional society. Searching for an alternative pattern of development, he began a serious study of Buddhism. One offspring of this search and research was his already classic paper, "Buddhist Economics."

Before expounding his ideas, it will help to spotlight the economic and ideological scenarios of many Third World countries right after the war. Many African and Asian countries were becoming politically independent with respect to the European metropolis. The new political leaders of these countries, as well as those of Latin America, aspired to promote the economic development of their nations. A relevant question posed by them to economists and other students of social life was: Is economic growth possible in a traditional society? With different degrees of qualifications, the prevailing answer was "yes." With the blessing of the national leaders and the funds of the international lending institutions, many countries embraced the path of economic growth based on the transfer of technologies and organizations utilized in the United States, Europe, and the Soviet Union. The pervading ideology was: Let us grow first, and later we will take care of the social distribution of income and the ecological impacts of growth.

Schumacher's advice for economic development in Burma corresponds with the best traditions of the economists of the German Historical School. These economists questioned the idea that there were natural laws of human behavior--as Adam Smith and other classical and neoclassical economists believed--and even less laws of historical development. Social theory, they thought, was related solely to a succession of prevailing circumstances; it was an expression of opinion--not a description of the world of nature. In a similar vein, Schumacher endeavored to investigate what would be a development style adequate for Burma--that is, for a Buddhist society and culture.

The Four Noble Truths of Buddhism are (1) there is sorrow in the becoming of life, (2) the cause of sorrow is desire (craving), (3) the way of overcoming sorrow is to overcome desire, and (4) the way of overcoming desire is to follow the Eightfold Path. One of the rules of the Eightfold Path is Right Livelihood. But economics is about livelihood, Schumacher thought--it is the way of satisfying human needs by means of an efficient use of resources. Then there must be something that could be called Buddhist Economics.

Within a Buddhist economy, the aim would be to satisfy basic human needs and then, according to the Four Noble Truths, to simplify desires and, therefore, to minimize luxury consumption. This is in contrast with the basic tenet of a hedonistic economy where an individual's welfare is believed to result from satisfaction of all possible needs and wants (desires). With regard to the two original resources--work and nature--a Buddhist economy will also be dealt with in a different way. In Western countries, the pervading idea is that work is a necessary evil. For Buddhism, instead, work gives man a chance to utilize and develop his faculties, enables him to overcome his ego-centeredness by relating with others and nature, and brings forth the goods and services needed for a becoming existence. Similarly, the products of nature--land, minerals, and forests--do not exist to be "exploited;" since they contribute to man's subsistence, they deserve a reverent and nonviolent manipulation.

These normative principles of the aims of an economic system indeed can be generalized to other societies and cultures. During his last visit to the University of California, Berkeley, Schumacher commented that he could have developed similar ideas investigating a "Gandhian Economics" or a "Gospel Economics" as well. Perhaps we can generalize even more and regard those ideas as the normative principles of an economics of "voluntary simplicity"--the movement toward frugality and self-reliance.

In 1962, Schumacher again went to the East--this time to advise the Planning Commission in Delhi on rural development programs. Here is where he conceived the concept, "intermediate technology." One can imagine the scenario that he found in India.

After Gandhi's death, Nehru tried to induce a process of economic growth patterned after the Soviet Union model--development of urban enclaves, industrialization, large-scale labor-saving technologies, and centralized planning. At the same time, the bulk of the population was living in rural areas and growing at a relatively fast rate, where the patterns of living and working were not only profoundly unsatisfactory but also in a process of accelerating decay.

Again, in a time when policymakers, international lending institutions, and most experts believed that "trickle down" effects of growth would take care of the needs of the poor, Schumacher was able to foresee that the problem of poverty in the rural areas and small towns had to be dealt with directly. He felt that it was necessary to by-pass the big cities and be directly concerned with the creation of an "agro-industrial structure" in the rural areas.

The task, he wrote, was to bring into existence millions of new work places in the areas where the people are living now and to design intermediate technologies--tools and equipment which are small, simple, low-capital cost, and nonviolent. This was similar to Gandhi's ideas about small-scale, home looms which helped the Indians to be self-sufficient in cloth making, and, thus, freer from British dominance. In Schumacher's view, smallness itself will allow the working process to be adapted to the organization level of local units. Simplicity will allow many local people to get started in a more productive process. Low-cost investments will allow more people and local institutions to invest in modern processes. Nonviolence will promote the production processes which work with nature instead of attempting to force them through natural systems.

Schumacher did not stop in the proposition of a new technological alternative but, after returning from India, committed himself to work for the diffusion of the concept and the actual design of intermediate technologies. In London in 1965, he started the "Intermediate Technology Development Group, Limited."

At home, in England, at the same time that he had the full-time job with the British Coal Board, he continued to give shape to his ideas about voluntary simplicity. During his spare time, he got involved in three major organizations. He founded and was an active member of the Soil Association which promotes organic farming. In 1957, he helped with the formation of the commonwealth of Scott Bader, a company run under the principles of worker self-management. As already mentioned, he started the Intermediate Technology group. Thus, Schumacher was a practical man whose mental work was oriented toward effective works.

He also traveled extensively throughout the world carrying his message to many people. He first toured America for this purpose in 1974. His last tour in this country was March, 1977. By this time, he had become an inspiration for the movement of voluntary simplicity in the United States. This time, he lectured at universities, visited small towns and farms, and even had a meeting with President Carter.

In September, 1977, while traveling from Geneva to Zurich, he became ill aboard a train and was taken to a hospital at Romont where he was pronounced dead on arrival. It is significant that this pilgrim--as he liked to see himself--began his journey into eternity traveling in a train. Even the silence of his death was a message for those working for new alternatives.

The retrospective exam of Schumacher's existence has exposed us to a multiplicity of experiences and ideas which have the virtue of refreshing our interest in living. But when these images phase out, what is left? What are the relevant teachings embodied by his life? I think that he, like other great beings, left for us both universal and contingent teachings--knowledge which is valid for most people and which likely will remain, and knowledge which is only applicable to a specific time, place, and people.

Let me begin with some of his contingent teachings. He was able to describe with clarity how the nature of a technology influences the modes of production exchange and consumption of a society. These economic activities, in turn, influence people's values and relationships. He then advocated the development and adoption of technologies, organizations, and consumption habits appropriate for a society which emulates the preservation and expansion of life--both material and spiritual life. In this vein, he conceived the idea of intermediate technology for poor communities of Third World countries. This claim for smallness was also well received by some people living in high industrial countries.

These ideas, however, did not go without challenges. Is smallness desirable? If it was, is smallness possible?

Schumacher's advocacy for intermediate technologies is a strong case for the overpopulated and poor communities of many Third World countries. Notice that intermediate technologies imply smallness with respect to the technological giantism being transferred from high industrialized countries to developing countries. But intermediate technologies do not necessarily imply smallness with regard to the traditional practices of impoverished peasant societies. He did not advocate the preservation of these practices but the development of technologies adequate for an even style of development.

The desirability of smallness within high industrial countries is open to more questions. It is not clear that the large-scale organizations and technologies developed, say, in the United States, could be replaced and still maintain the existing levels of material and cultural well-being. However, I think that there is a place for smallness in these countries if freedom and creativity are going to be emulated. Whether this smallness is possible depends more on the will to work of the people attracted by the idea, in the design of appropriate supporting institutions and, paradoxically, in some technological breakthroughs. Innovations in the field of electronics, computer sciences, communication, and even biological sciences may open the road toward more decentralized working processes. Furthermore, Schumacher's message should not be reduced to the criterion of smallness. His was more a pledge of adequateness of the working process to the human needs.

Schumacher thought that the way people produce their material subsistence has a large influence on their relationships and their notions of being. Therefore, he summoned up individuals and local communities to improve their ways of living and being by taking control of their working and home conditions--control on what and how to produce and consume. This way was challenged by those who think that a substantial change within the economic and social dimension of human life will only be possible after a change in the political and legal institutions of a society. They thought of Schumacher as an Utopian. In Good Work, his answer was:

> "I can't myself raise the winds that might blow us, or that ship, into a better world. But I can at least put up the sail so that when the winds come, I can catch it."

Now, what are the aspects of Schumacher's life and ideas which are universal enough as to be teachings for us? I can identify four major ones: the importance of having an integral view of life, the idea of living with measure, commitment to life, and a good sense of humor.

Schumacher's ability to foresee the cultural and social consequences of alternative ways of living and working were not derived from a specialized field of knowledge. He had a comprehensive view of the whole system. This comprehensive view, in turn, was not only the result of the aggregation of information and an expertise in many disciplines but also, and perhaps more important, the result of wisdom. This wisdom springs out of the individual who know himself. Quoting from the Tao de Jing of Lao Tzu, Schumacher wrote:

> "He who knows others is wise.
> He who knows himself is enlightened."

His concepts about smallness, intermediate technologies, and the use of natural resources underwent a process of precipitation. By the end of his life, they could be reduced to the rule of living with measure. He said that we could say that the art of living is to maintain a sense of proportion in our lives.

Schumacher yearned for shaping his ideas into works. He felt the call to be committed to life, and he answered this call with a passion for effectiveness. He was a person who could think globally and act locally. He was fond of the following example: say we are told that there are 8 million unemployed in the United States. The size of the problem paralyzes our imagination and we can do nothing. But it would be different if we were told that there are, for example, 90 unemployed in our neighborhood. We could then focus on the problem, find out who they are, what we can do, and what they want to do. It is only when things are located at the proper human scale that they become manageable.

Many great teachers are humorous as a way of communicating their ideas. Schumacher was not an exception. In Good Work, he wrote:

> "With a name like mine (Shu-macher), I find it easy to understand that to be a good shoemaker it is not enough to know a lot about making shoes; you also have to know about feet. The shoe made for the big fellow does not fit the foot of the little fellow. The small foot needs a different shoe, not an inferior one but one of the right size."

Thus, some of Schumacher's ideas may prove to be effective for some people, in some places and at some time, and perhaps less effective for other people in other places and time. But the universal teachings that he embodied will always blaze the trail for those who work for the preservation and expansion of life.

Based on the presentation by Carlos A. Benito. Opening quotation from E. F. Schumacher, A Guide for the Perplexed.

References and Recommended Readings

Schumacher, Ernest Fritz. A Guide for the Perplexed. New York: Harper and Row, 1977.

_____. Good Work. New York: Harper and Row, 1979.

_____. Small is Beautiful: Economics as if People Mattered. New York: Harper and Row, 1973.

ALBERT EINSTEIN
Thinker

> *The fairest thing we can experience is the mysterious. It is the fundamental emotion which stands at the cradle of true art and true science.*

Albert Einstein is perhaps the most famous scientist of this century. His work in physics and the development of the Theory of Relativity revolutionized our way of thinking abut the world. When we think of Albert Einstein, the image which immediately comes to mind is that of the prototypical, absent-minded scientist. The characteristic pictures of Einstein with his wild hair and rumpled clothes add to our impression of him as a man so preoccupied with theoretical problems that he had little concern for the details of daily life.

In many ways, this impression is an accurate reflection of Einstein. Those who have known or met Einstein are full of humorous anecdotes about this absent-minded scientist who was often oblivious to things which routinely concern other people. Along with this stereotyped image of Einstein, we often think of him as the quintessential genius, a man whose intellectual powers place him in a category so unreachable to us that we monumentalize this aspect and forget the human qualities which made Einstein the type of person he was.

I wish to concentrate not on Einstein the "super-human" genius but rather on those aspects of his life and ideas which we can learn from and admire. Einstein's lifework merits our respect and admiration not only because of the immense contribution he made to scientific knowledge but because it is a reflection of his attitudes and philosophy. A brief chronology of the major events in his life outlines his views and ideas on a variety of subjects beyond the scientific which reflects his general philosophy.

Albert Einstein was born in Ulm, Germany, in 1879. He was educated in Germany and Switzerland. His family immigrated to Northern Italy when he was a teenager. When he was 16, he renounced his German citizenship and became a Swiss citizen. His childhood was not especially unusual and he showed no particular signs of extraordinary intellectual development. The only notable event in his early development was his lateness in acquiring language proficiency. It is said he really did not begin to speak fluently until he was nine years old. From an early age, Einstein avoided accepting prescribed facts and ways of thinking. He did not readily believe the types of things most of us take for granted and even as an adult he questioned everything with an almost childlike innocence. Of his development Einstein has said that he often asked himself how it came to be that he was the one to develop the theory of relativity. The reason, he decided, was that normal adults never stop to consider the problems of space and time. But his own development had been so delayed that he began to wonder about space and time only after he had grown up. Naturally, then, he could go deeper into the problem than could a child with normal abilities.

Einstein was not particularly successful in school. He had difficulty conforming to the rules of the school and the demands of his teachers. He attended University at a technical school in Zurich, Switzerland. He studied physics and planned to become a teacher. However, he could not secure a teaching position after his graduation. Through the help of a friend he eventually found work in a patent office in Bern, Switzerland. After work he continued to work at home on physics problems and to meet with students to tutor them and converse about physics and philosophy. Einstein married a classmate named Mileva, and they had two children.

He eventually began publishing papers in physics journals. In 1905, he published a paper which outlined his Special Theory of Relativity. This unconventional paper proved to be the cornerstone which revolutionized physics and changed man's perceptions of the universe. The paper dealt with problems in the conception of space and time which Einstein had been contemplating since his youth. In its most basic sense, Einstein's Theory of Relativity proposed that there was no absolute time or absolute space by which to measure, but rather that these constructs would vary according to their relative positions.

As Einstein's scientific work became more widely respected, he became an important figure in European scientific circles. He did research and teaching in Czechoslovakia, Switzerland, Holland, and Germany. His theory of relativity was discussed not only among scientists but among the general public as well. People around the world began to realize the importance of Einstein's work and developed a deep admiration and respect for "Mr. Relativity." Within a short time, he leapt from his position as an obscure civil servant in Switzerland to messiah-like fame. He received invitations from around the world to discuss his theory. He traveled throughout Europe, Japan, and the United States speaking to crowds of enthusiastic listeners.

Einstein was never one to relish fame and glory and preferred to continue his work with the minimum of distractions. He moved to Berlin and continued his research. He lived there until 1933 when he was forced to leave Germany due to the rise of anti-Semitism. He came to the United States and spent the remaining 20 years of his life at Princeton University.

One striking aspect of Einstein's character is the humbleness he maintained in light of all his achievements and the international fame bestowed upon him. In all of his accomplishments he never took personal credit or attached any personal pride to them. He realized that anything which may be credited to him was only possible because of the work of others. In The World as I See It, he writes:

> "A hundred times everyday I remind myself that my inner and outer life depend on the labours of other men, living and dead, and that I must exert myself in order to give in the same measure as I have received and am still receiving."

He was always prepared to abandon an idea or theory he had when it was proved inadequate. He never presumed that his ideas or theories were ultimate explanations.

He extended his belief in the interdependencies among all things to the political realm. He was always a strong proponent of internationalism and detested the artificial barriers of nations which separated people or made them feel superior or inferior. After World War I, Einstein worked within the European scientific community trying to build links of cooperation and understanding among scientists who were also influential in the politics of their respective countries. Einstein was also a deeply committed pacifist and believed that the creation of an international league of nations was the only way to prevent conflict.

In 1922 Einstein was invited to join the International Committee on Intellectual Cooperation, a group which intended to combine some of the most respected thinkers of the time to cooperate in areas which affected world peace. Einstein, at first, wholeheartedly accepted the invitation to join the committee. After a while, however, he became disillusioned with its operations. The delegates were seen as representatives of their countries and Einstein was in the awkward position of representing Germany although he did not feel any particular German allegiance. He was disappointed that the Committee should be structured along nationalistic lines and further disappointed when it became apparent the league was doing little to accomplish its goals. After a while, Einstein resigned from the Committee.

Einstein was also called upon to support the Zionist movement in Europe during the 1920s. While he never felt a particularly strong personal identification with his Jewish heritage, he agreed with the cause of setting up a Jewish state in Palestine. He was especially interested in the formation of the Hebrew University. He toured the United States, speaking to crowds across the country in an effort to raise funds for the Hebrew University. He maintained a low profile in the Zionist movement, often conflicting with more ardent Zionists on the treatment of Arabs in Palestine. Just as Einstein did not like to separate people among nationalities, he also did not like the separation of people along religious lines.

There has been much confusion over Einstein's religious and spiritual views. When his theory of relativity was first popularized, it was attacked by some theologians as anti-God or anti-religion. In fact, Einstein had deep spiritual beliefs which in no way conflicted with his scientific work. He believed that the physical world was created by God in an orderly and harmonious way and that the scientist's work was merely man's attempt to understand and unravel the way the universe was put together. Einstein's God thus stood for an orderly system of universal laws which could be discovered by human beings who had the courage and the imagination to do so. What Einstein deplored about organized religions is that they often set up artifical systems of reward and punishment and separated people instead of uniting them.

Throughout his life, Einstein avoided identifying too closely with any group. He developed his ideas and approach to life without attaching himself to roles of nationality, religion, or occupation. His striving to transcend artifically imposed classifications and categories permeates not only his scientific work but his attitude of human relationships. He wrote that he never belonged to his country, his home, his friends, or his immediate family with his whole heart, but that he always had an "obstinate sense of detachment" and the need for solitude throughout his life.

There are many things to be learned from the life of Albert Einstein beyond his scientific contributions. He lived his life in a way consistent with his ideas and views of the world. He participated in life with a sense of humility and a cognizance of the interrelationships and interdependencies which exist in all realms of life. In The World As I See It, he leave us with a sense of this often overlooked side of himself:

> "The true value of a human being is determined primarily by the measure and the sense in which he has attained true liberation from the self."

Based on the presentation by Sandra Rowland. Opening quotation from Albert Einstein, The World As I See It.

References and Recommended Readings

Clark, Ronald W. Einstein: The Life and Times. New York: Avon Books, 1971.

Einstein, Albert. <u>The World As I See It</u>. New York:
The Philosophical Library, 1949.

MOTHER TERESA
Instrument of Love

"The biggest disease today is not leprosy
or tuberculosis, but rather the feeling of
being unwanted, uncared for and deserted
by everybody. The greatest evil is the
lack of love and charity, the terrible
indifference towards one's neighbor who
lives at the roadside assaulted by exploitation, corruption, poverty and disease."

Mother Teresa, the simple Catholic nun from
India who received the Nobel Peace Prize of 1979, is
a universal being whose life offers us many lessons
about faith and participation through her unique gift
for fusing prayer and work.

She was born to Albanian parents in Czechoslovakia in 1910. Her family was peasant stock, her
father a grocer. A spiritual mentor of hers attri-
buted her "tough and revolutionary manner" to her
Albanian heritage: If the structures stood in the way
of fulfilling her ideas, she'd change them.

As a schoolgirl she was caught up in the missionary activities being carried out in India and became
active in a lay support group. She had felt an early
stirring in her soul, and as the years passed, she
realized that although she had no desire to leave her

family--she had a very happy family and a good life--she needed to respond to that inner call and give more of herself. She went first to Dublin to join the Sisters of Loreto and then to India in 1929. She spent the two years of her novitiate in Darjeeling. She took her first vows in 1931 and her final vows in 1937.

For the next 20 years she taught high school to upper and middle-class Indian and English girls in a cloistered setting in Calcutta. She taught geography and history and later served as principal. From all accounts, she was a very gifted teacher who deeply touched her students. Again, she had a very beautiful life--the school's walls contained lovely gardens and offered a peaceful existence--even though they bordered the noise and chaos of Calcutta's worst slums. So the work of these 20 years was very different from the life she later took up.

In 1946, Mother Teresa experienced a second calling. She was on a train to Darjeeling, bound for retreat. She had begun to feel some of the limitations of the work and the place of her teaching with the Sisters of Loreto. Some of her students had been volunteering in the neighboring slums, and she responded with a growing need to give more of herself. So, at age 36, another call: "the message was quite clear. I was to leave the convent and help the poor while living among them. It was an order. I knew where I belonged but I did not know how to get there."

We tend to begin with a snapshot view of the lives of great beings. We know them only by their accomplishments, by their great deeds. And here is a woman in her mid-thirties who felt a call to leave a comfortable, secure existence where she was well loved and respected. Yet, she experienced a call to give up all of these comforts, her community, everything she had known, and to take on another work that would demand tremendous sacrifice. Throughout all of this, she never doubted. She knew what she had to do--though she had no idea how to begin. She certainly had no idea that in 20 years, there would be 30 houses in 50 countries--she knew only that she had to respond to that call.

She returned to Calcutta and applied for permission to be relieved of her vows, to leave cloistered life. She had to wait for two years. This was a real test of her faith and her obedience. She did not flee or rebel, she took the next step, and she did this within the structure of the Church. The day the permission was granted, she left, wearing a coarse white cotton sari, of the same cloth worn by the poorest of the poor--a white sari with a blue border and a cross fastened to her shoulder. She had no money, took few possessions. She had no idea what she would do or how to proceed. First, she went to study medicine with the Sisters of Patna, because she wanted to be able to help the poor more directly than her teaching skills would allow.

A few months later, in December of 1946, she returned to Calcutta and lived with a family there. On her first day back, she left the house, gathered about her a few children from the street and began to teach them the simplest elements of health and a few letters of the alphabet.

In a city of millions, full of human suffering, she simply began. She performed no survey of the needs of the people, created no bureaucracy, no forms, no evaluations. She merely collected five children near the compound in which she was staying and began to

work with them, responding to their needs. One
woman alone, living among the poorest of the poor.

Within a year, she was joined by one of her
former students. Many of the early Sisters had been
taught by her--a testament to the strength of her
example. Within two years, there were 12 Sisters,
and they were given the designation of a diocesan
congregation. The work grew. Soon there were
hundreds of children in schools and shelters for the
abandoned and crippled children. No child was turned
away. There was always an extra bed. No one in
need was denied assistance.

Much has been written about the work with the
dying. The story of how that work began reveals
much about Mother Teresa. She was walking on the
street in Calcutta and came upon a woman, dying and
half eaten by rats. She picked her up and took her to
the municipal hospital. There they waited and waited
and waited and no help was forthcoming. So, Mother
Teresa went directly to the local authorities saying
that there was a need for a place for the dying to
receive care. Within 24 hours, she was offered an
empty building adjacent to a Hindu temple. The
building had served as a resting place for those who
came to worship the goddess Kali. Mother Teresa
responded, "This will do fine." She and the sisters
cleaned the building, and Kaligat--the Home for the
Dying--opened two days later. This was 1952.

This story illustrates how Mother Teresa acts:
simply, directly, without hesitation. She sees a need
and responds. She inspires by her own willingness to
take on what is hard, to give her all.

In 1957, the work expanded to include service to
those suffering from the ravages of leprosy. Again,
Mother Teresa was able to respond to the need of the

moment. The local government was trying to evict a leper settlement to make way for a new development. The people of the colony appealed to Mother Teresa to help them find a home. She intervened on their behalf and within a week found a new place for them.

The works of the Missionaries of Charity continued to expand throughout Calcutta and to other cities in India. Under church law, they could not grow beyond the borders of India for ten years. So this period was a time of building within, of training and strengthening the Sisters. A need arose for men to help the Sisters in their work of caring for the intimate needs of the dying and, in 1962, the Missionary Brothers were founded. Today, there are over 250 brothers involved in the work. In 1965, the Missionaries of Charity became a pontifical congregation, an honor usually accorded only after 40 or 50 years of service.

Many have joined themselves to the work of Mother Teresa: Co-workers, a lay support group; The Sick and Suffering, who offer their prayres; and The Contemplatives, cloistered nuns who pray for their sisters on the outside. By now, the work has expanded to over 25 cities in India and to more than 50 countries in the world. There are 1,800 nuns, and 250 brothers, and over 120,000 Co-workers in a chain of love around the world.

Mother Teresa practices a very practical form of mysticism: while others talk, she works; while others put forth questions, she solves problems. She has a sense of what is real and urgent.

She is guided by a deep faith. If the work is meant to be, it will prosper; if not, it will die. She does not worry about risks or the prospect of failure, she only works.

In the fall of 1979, Mother Teresa was awarded the Nobel Peace Prize in recognition that poverty, hunger, and disease also constitute a threat to peace. With characteristic humility, she accepted in the name of the poor.

The way in which the Sisters of the Missionaries of Charity live also offers lessons in love for us. Their vow is to give "wholehearted service to the poorest of the poor" and to live among those they serve, to share their poverty. They have few possessions: two saris, one to wash, one to wear; a shining metal bucket for washing; and a pair of sandals. All around the world, they awake at 4:30 a.m., celebrating Mass, joining in prayer. Then, clad in their coarse white cotton sari, with blue border and cross at their shoulder, they go out, prepared to respond to the needs of the poor.

The spirit of the Society has three aspects: total surrender, loving trust, and cheerfulness. Total surrender is to become an instrument of God, to empty oneself of personal desires, to be free to be a channel for divine love, to offer oneself completely. At a time when the Catholic Church has been having trouble attracting postulants, the Missionaries of Charity continue to grow. Perhaps the hard life, the necessity of giving up so much speaks to a genuine need in young people to offer themselves. Loving trust is faith in the divine. In each house of the Sisters of Charity, there is a quotation from the Bible, "I thirst." Their work is to quench the thirst of Jesus for love.

Although their activities resemble those carried out by governments and charitable agencies, their work is not a social work. Mother Teresa once explained, "Welfare is for a purpose, our work is for the person." It is a means to express their love in a very practical way, to "serve Jesus in his most distressing disguise."

Cheerfulness is to attend not only to the physical needs of the people, but to make them feel loved and wanted, to discover and enhance their dignity and beauty. Even if only for a few hours, it is to care for the dying, to clean them, to minister to them with love and tenderness, that they may know they are loved.

The success of these works is judged not by its impact on decreasing the poverty and suffering--their efforts are but a drop of water in the ocean of need--but by the degree of their giving, by the measure of their giving of themselves.

Asked what was most important in the training of the Sisters, Mother Teresa replied, "Silence is the most important thing in their training; the silence of humility, of charity; the silence of the eyes, of the ears, of the tongue. There is no life of prayer without silence." This process of emptying themselves, of seeking and dwelling in interior silence is a crucial touchstone of their work.

And all of the work of the Missionaries of Charity has grown out of the faith and conviction of one lone soul who decided to live her life in harmony with her vocation.

Mother Teresa was 36 years old before she began the work by which we know her, so perhaps our own lives have surprises in store for us. Few of us are likely to achieve her impact on the world, but we still can learn from her example.

Perhaps what stands out the strongest is her incredible faith. She does not doubt, and this allows her to be single-minded in a very dynamic way; it lends a force and momentum which propels a soul like her, who is open enough to hear a call and strong enough to respond to it. Mother Teresa had no idea where her life would take her, she only knew that she had to keep working to fulfill that vocation, however it might express itself. The Missionaries follow no program, offer no packaged solutions--they only respond to what the needs of the poor seem to be. They go to work and to serve.

Many of us may feel there is something which should be done, but we have so many conflicting notions about what is important on a given day and so many considerations about a given action. Mother Teresa continually pared that away until what moved her was very simple but very compelling and obviously strong enough to inspire others to join with her in that work.

Another striking quality about Mother Teresa is her humility. She did not begin as a famous, charismatic world leader. She is a very ordinary person, born of peasant stock. Little in her early years would have predicted what fruits her faith would bear. She is a luminous being, a beacon to many; this comes from having continually scraped away the layers so that her special light could shine out. All of us have that light, that spark--it remains for us to polish ourselves. For such strong leadership to come from one so profoundly humble is almost a paradox. The gentleness and kindness so many have described is proportionate to the way in which she has emptied herself.

There is a wonderful story that illustrates her faith and humility. A wealthy banker came to her demanding to know where she found the money for her various projects. Mother Teresa asked him how he had found his way to her. He answered that he had felt an urge to offer himself to her. She smiled and replied, "Well, that is my budget." She trusts that if God means for the work to be carried out, the resources will appear. She extends this belief to the life of the congregation itself. If it is based only on her personal charisma, it will die with her. If it is based on a spark which has ignited other souls who burn as true, then the work will go on.

Finally, we can learn from her example of participation, the joining of love to action. There is no distance between helper and helped. She reaches out, not because they are pitiful; rather, she serves them because they are truly worthy of love and caring. Each person has the spark of the divine and deserves love. She does not worry about being effective, only about giving all that she has to give. People criticize the smallness of the effort in the face of such great need, and she responds that it is a drop in the ocean, but if that drop were not in the ocean, then the ocean would be a little less.

The work is in the Gandhian tradition. The Sisters live simply. They are poor and frugal in their ways. They are mobile, able to respond quickly to requests for assistance because they have pared down their needs to so little. The work is not defined by where they are or what they do or whom they are accustomed to serving--service is offered wherever there is need. Mother Teresa has, for the most part, avoided the politics, although her work has been a force. Her work has been with the poorest of the poor. She teaches self-help and encourage the use of local resources. She is nothing if not pragmatic. If people have no way to earn a living except to beg, she inquires after their success at the end of the day.

Below is the prayer recited daily by all Sisters and Co-workers around the world. Perhaps it will serve to link us to the work of Mother Teresa.

Make us worthy, Lord, to serve our fellow men throughout the world who live and die in poverty and hunger. Give them, through our hands, this day their daily bread, and by our understanding love give Peace and Joy.

Lord, make me a channel of Thy peace, that where there is hatred I may bring love; that where there is wrong, I may bring the spirit of forgiveness; that where there is discord, I may bring harmony; that where there is error, I may bring truth; that where there is doubt, I may bring faith; that where there is despair, I may bring hope; that where there are shadows, I may bring light; that where there is sadness, I may bring joy.

Lord, grant that I may seek rather to comfort than to be comforted; to understand than to be understood; to love than to be loved; for it is by forgetting self that one finds; it is by dying that one awakens to eternal life. Amen.

Based on the presentation by Laura Peck.
Opening quotation from Malcolm Muggeridge, <u>Something Beautiful for God</u>.

(Internal quotations from <u>Servant of Love</u>.)

References and Recommended Readings

Doig, Desmond. <u>Mother Teresa: Her People and Her Work</u>. London: Collins, 1976.

Le Joly, E. <u>Servant of Love</u>. San Francisco: Harper and Row, 1977.

McGovern, James. <u>To Give the Love of Christ: A Portrait of Mother Teresa and the Missionaries of Charity</u>. New York: Paulist Press, 1978.

Muggeridge, Malcolm. <u>Something Beautiful for God</u>. New York: Harper and Row, 1971.

Part Two

THE ART OF WALKING

Words guide . . .
Examples move . . .
But only giving of oneself transforms.

Santiago Bovisio

THE ART OF WALKING

*The longest journey starts
with just one step.*

Lao Tzu, <u>Tao de Jing</u>

To walk is to be human. No other creature on this earth walks as we do. Since we first learned to stand upright, we have walked the world, walking with many intents and purposes. We walked in search of grains to gather. We walked looking for better hunting grounds. We walked to find water supplies, fishing rivers, trading posts, to establish villages, and to build cities. Walking has always been our primary mode of transportation. Over the centuries we have devised many vehicles to aid our travel, but in spite of this, we still need to walk to attain basic mobility. From the moment we step out of bed in the morning, we begin the day by walking.

Although walking is still basic to our daily activities, we moderns have developed a different relationship with it. Because of our emphasis on mechanized modes of transportation, our attitude toward walking has become one of avoidance. So much in the habit are we of jumping into our car for every errand that we even do so to go a block to a nearby store. City dwellers are notorious for taking a taxi rather than walking two blocks. Because we have developed faster and easier means of transportation, we have organized in our attitudes the idea that these means are always better.

Recent years have brought a questioning of our basic technology-induced values, bringing about a revolution in attitudes toward health, diet, and exercise. Walking, quite naturally, fits well into the back-to-nature emphasis that has been rising recently. This change has come about because there is something essential to the human being that our industrial society has tended to ignore.

To better understand how walking relates to our basic needs is to place walking within the context of the complete human being. A complete human being is made up of a body, soul, and spirit. The body, with its physical form, its functions, and its senses, is said to be the vehicle of the soul. The soul is the home of the intellectual and emotional activities, and it acts as the vehicle of the spirit. The spirit is the divine essence of the human being. For the whole person, then, walking can have many functions, harmoniously relating to these three parts of our being.

One can walk for health, that is, to develop and maintain the physical fitness of the body. One can walk for meaning, enhancing intellectual possibilities and purifying the feelings of the soul. One can also walk to reflect or meditate, to deepen an understanding of the spiritual life. Thus, walking becomes the Art of Walking, taking on different dimensions in relationship to the complete human being.

The ways of walking are many, from daily walking programs, easy sauntering and Sunday strolling, to vigorous hiking and backpacking excursions. We are inclined to dismiss no form of walking. We think that walking, besides being an excellent exercise for physical fitness, is at the same time one of the best means for uniting with nature, for practicing human conviviality, for learning, for recollecting, for meditating, and for opening ourselves to the Divine Presence.

WALKING FOR HEALTH

With the current renewed interest in health in this country, many people have been searching for better and more efficient ways of exercising. The jogging craze of the last decade is perhaps the most famous example of this effort. We have all become aware of the need for exercise: to benefit our cardiovascular system, ease tension, strengthen our muscles and body tone; but not all of us know which is the best form of exercise to choose. Jogging certainly is not suitable for everyone. It is not recommended for those over 45 who have not had a regular exercise program for some time; it is not good for those with back, leg, or bone problems because of the stress it produces to the system; and it is not at all recommended for those who have recently recovered from heart attacks. However, there is one form of exercise that is recommend for these people as well as for all people: walking. The President's Council on Physical Fitness and Sports has said: "Walk every chance you get. Walking is actually one of the best all-around physical activities."

Exercising the heart and lungs is essential for any physical fitness program. This kind of exercise is known as aerobics, which comes from the Greek meaning "oxygen" or "air." Aerobic exercises include jogging, running, swimming, dancing, and walking. We have the tendency to think that the exercises that are the hardest to do are the most efficient in achieving good health. But actually we have learned that this is not the case. Through the experiments of Dr. Kenneth Cooper, conducted during the 1960s, it was learned that there was absolute equality between the different types of aerobic exercises. Walkers, he proved, are as physically fit as runners or swimmers. The important thing to accomplish in exercise is to elevate the heart rate and stimulate circulation. Walking accomplishes this as well as any other exercise.

The idea of walking for exercise is to walk at a speed that raises the heart beat up to more than double its normal rate and to retain it at this higher level for 30 minutes, every day if possible, but no less than four times a week. In this way, the heart and lungs get the full benefit of exercise, excessive fat is burned off, and the capacity to process oxygen and purify the blood is greatly improved. A very scientific way to go about taking one's pulse and documenting one's exercise is outlined in Dr. Marchetti's Walking Book which is listed in the Sources at the end of this chapter. He demonstrates very well how walking is a superior exercise since it achieves good health without the risks associated with some of the more strenuous exercises: shin splints, strained muscles, tennis elbow, etc.

Another health problem that many have in this country is that of being overweight. Walking, especially in combination with a proper diet, is an excellent and painless weight reducer. It not only burns up calories, but it helps to alleviate the "hunger" brought on by tension and boredom. No diet should be without some form of exercise to tighten up loose muscles and to hasten the burning of calories.

Improved circulation, increased heart and lung capacity, reduced tension, good mental health and well-being, weight control, and longevity are all benefits of a constant and continuous walking program. Because of its ease and gentleness for persons of all ages and physical health, it remains one of the best exercises available.

WALKING FOR MEANING

Walking is an excellent means for reflecting, recollecting, meditating, and learning. In this way, walking as a physical activity can be integrated with the mental activities of the human being. Walking is also a wonderful social activity if it is done as a group project. The series, Walking with Contemplation, combined the mental and social aspects of walking by incorporating walking with the study of the lives of great beings. Walking became a way of learning, of finding meaning. Throughout history, people have used walking to find meaning in their lives. One of these ways is the age-old pilgrimage.

Pilgrimages, in the original sense of the word, are journeys to a shrine, holy place, or to a place of historical interest. Most often, pilgrims walk together to these places on foot. But the holy places that a pilgrim journeys to do not need to have religious significance or historical interest. You and a group of friends can hike anywhere with the intention of pilgrimage. You can participate, for example, on a group pilgrimage with the purpose of a retreat. On retreat, one can explore more transcendent ideas, such as: What is the meaning of my life? How can we help others? What is the true vocation of my life? and so on. During pilgrimages, the exercise of walking and the contact with nature help the soul to disattach herself from her habitual preoccupations and to concentrate on a more transcendent subject.

Most pilgrimages require a method and guidance from a person who, besides knowing the art of walking, knows even better how to traverse the path of life. A good leader is essential. A pilgrimage can last for one day or involve an overnight stay extending to several days if so desired. The method for a one-day pilgrimage can be the following: A group of pilgrims meet early in the morning. Everyone brings the necessary walking equipment already decided upon and knows some techniques of walking (see the following section). In addition, each pilgrim has received from their guide a schedule listing the different physical and mental activities of the journey. Before striking out, the guide makes a short invocation. All begin walking as a group, trying to stay together throughout the whole journey. Depending on their schedule, they will spend some hours in silence, meditation, sightseeing, and dialogue. During the major breaks, the guide makes a presentation about an inspiring life or idea (as in the series, Walking with Contemplation). There is time for communal meals and collective work, preparing meals, and cleaning up. And in so doing, the day takes on a real rhythm, with a time and place for everything.

Pilgrimages and retreats can be organized by families, groups of friends, co-workers, couples, students of a school or college, church members, and so on. They are an extraordinary means of looking at our lives with a broader perspective, learning how to live, and improving relationships.

A GUIDING PRINCIPLE

With walking, as with other aspects of your daily
life, transform your actions into a practice for
integral unfoldment, remembering this guiding
principle: Work in a conscious, continuous, and
scrupulous way.

PROGRAMS FOR DAILY WALKING

One of the best things about walking is the freedom and flexibility for individual methods that it allows. It is a simple exercise available to just about everybody: one does not need to have a special athletic prowess, nor does it require long, detailed study of technique and form. In fact, a walking program can be as simple as this: walk every chance you get, every day.

If one likes, one can follow a more formal or precise method and keep a detailed account of one's progress. Keeping a journal of your observations and progress may be beneficial to maintaining interest in your new program.

If one is in poor physical condition or has been rather sedentary for some time, it is a good idea to see a doctor before beginning any exercise program, even a walking one. Although easy, walking is still exercise and can be overdone. One needs an outlined, progressive program. What follows are some general guidelines and ideas to help you get started in walking, but a walking program can be freely designed and adjusted to each one's individual circumstances.

As an exercise program, plan when you will walk, then set up a routine, and most importantly, be faithful to your chosen method. Set aside a specific amount of time for walking daily, say, 30 minutes, and stick with it. Most experts recommend daily walking but, if time is a problem, a long and vigorous walk four times a week is considered sufficient.

Begin thinking in terms of walking. Replace other modes of transportation with walking as much as possible. For example, structure a walking program along with your daily routine of commuting to work. If you ride the bus, walk to the second or third bus stop from your home and get off the bus two or three stops before work, walking the rest of the way. If you drive, park the car several blocks away from work (this often has the added advantage of finding a parking place more easily if your work place is a crowded one). Walking on your lunch hour gives renewed vitality for the remainder of the afternoon's work. Walk a half an hour or so after dinner. Look for every opportunity to walk: use the stairs instead of the elevator. Walk to the store instead of driving. Set aside the time to walk to visit friends. Walking can become an unconscious good habit if we consciously set out with the intention of changing our old way of living.

Walking Techniques: How to Walk

Walking is the most natural exercise of all. Even without suggestions on walking techniques, one's style would be improved simply by walking more. The most important thing to remember in walking is posture. Walk tall and straight, arms relaxed and swinging at your side, carrying nothing in your hands (always use a backpack for carrying your supplies). Find a natural rhythm, thinking about breathing smoothly and consistently with a count of your steps. Breathing is vital in conserving energy while exercising and for reaping all the benefits from the exercise:

not only are the leg muscles strengthened, but the cardiovascular system is as well.

In walking for exercise, it is important to walk with a fast, yet comfortable pace. Try to keep a consistent pace while walking, whether on level ground, uphill, or downhill. This helps achieve grace and control, and to strengthen those muscles that rebel on steep inclines. Think often of stretching your leg muscles while walking; try consistently to take longer--yet comfortable--steps. The body's own natural rhythm will eventually take over, and you will know when you are walking correctly.

The ancient Greeks thought that the walking technique was very important and had a practice of teaching their young the proper posture, stature, and grace that should accompany walking. Native Americans knew the importance of walking with silent grace, and hunting expeditions in the forests often included a review of walking correctly. So even though walking comes quite naturally to us, there is something to be learned about the best way to achieve a good walking style.

A good set of stretching exercises before beginning your daily walk is essential to prepare the body and mind for the change in pace. The American Medical Association has developed a set of exercises which are convenient for walkers as they can be performed while standing. They include head and neck exercises, arm exercises, trunk exercises, leg exercises, and cardiopulmonary exercises. The same exercises are highly recommended for warming down as well. But perhaps no better exercise for walkers exists than Yoga. Hatha yoga techniques prepare all of one's body through a system of complete stretches. It is also ideal for learning to develop proper breath-

201

ing control which is so important to walkers. Many good books exist on the market for basic Yoga, and classes are often held in local colleges and adult education centers around the country.

Walking Equipment and Apparel

By far the most important piece of equipment for walking is a pair of good walking shoes. Good, sturdy, and yet comfortable shoes are a must. A good shoe should have a wide, flat heel, a broad, rounded toe, and a cushioned inner sole. Your shoes should be loose enough so that you can turn your toe under when you have them on. At the same time, it should not be so loose as to rub and blister the foot. For long day hikes or overnight backpacking trips, it is vital that shoes be well broken in. Give those new shoes a chance around town before taking them out on a long hike.

Second in importance to shoes are socks. Cotton ones are excellent as they promote good circulation and are nonallergetic. Wool socks are a good alternative in winter months, but should have a cotton underlining to avoid itching and scratching. It is often a good idea to wear two pairs of socks when walking for long distances to help prevent blistering and sore feet.

In the case of hiking, the list of equipment is longer. For a one-day hike you will need a backpack and in it the following:

A lightweight poncho.
A canteen and cup.
A field guidebook, a copy of Walking with Contemplation, or other reading material.

Extra socks.
A tote litter bag.
Lunch.
Camera and film.
Binoculars.
Kleenex.
First aid kit.

In your pockets you can carry:

Adhesive bandages.
Compass and map.
Matches.
Knife and string.
Pad and pencil.
Telephone dime.
A whistle.

Over your body wear:

Appropriate clothing depending on weather.
Walking or hiking shoes.
Socks.
Hat.
Wristwatch.

Depending on your hiking style, you may also want to carry a walking stick.

Even on short hikes, be sure that your canteen is full of water, iced tea, or unsweetened fruit juices. Fruit juices contain natural sugars which boost your energy.

Hikers need a lot of energy and should carry a good nutritious snack. Gorp is an old favorite among children, and few adults will complain about it either!

Recipe for Gorp:

> 1 cup peanuts.
> 1 cup raisins.
> 1 cup candy-coated chocolates.

Mix all ingredients together and package it in individual bags for each hiker. You can substitute or add sunflower seeds, shredded coconut, and any kinds of nuts or chopped fruits for added protein and vitamin value.

For lunch, you may decide between cooking or bringing your own food. Experienced hikers usually bring a sack lunch, some fruit, and a hot or cold soup in a vacuum thermos. Still, a simpler trail lunch is one or two apples, three or four slices of cheese, a small box of raisins, and some fig bars.

If you decide to backpack or camp, the list of needed equipment and know-how is larger and more specialized. We suggest you consult some of the available books on the subject. Two good books that you most likely will find in a public library are The Official Boy Scout Handbook and the Fieldbook of the Boy Scouts of America. Although written for boys and girls, or perhaps because of this, you will find thorough details for backpacking and camping life. Besides these books, there exist many other good works, some of them listed in our Sources at the end of this section. Additional equipment for backpacking as compared with hiking is: well-broken-in hiking boots, additional pair of sneakers, backpack, sleeping bag, air mattress or foam pad, ground cloth, tent, stove, cooking and eating utensils, change of clothing, lighter weight (freeze dried) food, and plenty of fresh water.

Music and Song of the Trail

We think that walking is more joyful and meaningful if it is done with silence, leaving radios and TV sets home during walks, hikes, and camping trips. Of course, besides sightseeing, exploring, meditating, and talking, some walkers enjoy music and singing. In this case you can bring along a flute or another small instrument and play your own music. Even if you do not play any small instrument, you can whistle. Whistling is one of the most ancient and natural ways of playing music. In the past, most people used to whistle with great musical skills. Futhermore, you can sing both solo or in chorus. Throughout the centuries, many beautiful songs of human fraternity, reverence for nature, and adoration for God have been created in outdoor places. Many walkers like to play or to sing during the sunrise and the sunset. It helps to put one in harmony with the natural currents of the day.

DISAPPEARANCE

Walk with respect and reverence for nature. Conscious walkers leave no signs that they have been in a wood, a mountain, a desert, a beach, or a street. They take all papers, wrappers, cans, and containers back home with them. Learn to disappear as a separate and possessive personality. We can assume responsibility for the preservation of our environment and for the well-being of all animal and human creatures. Participate through the practice of disappearance.

SOURCES AND SUGGESTED READINGS

Davis, John T. Walking. Kansas City: Andrew and McMeel, Inc., 1979.

Fletcher, Colin. The New Complete Walker. New York: Alfred A. Knopp, Inc., 1967.

Gale, Bill. The Wonderful World of Walking. New York: William Morrow and Co., Inc., 1967.

Goode, Ruth and Aaron Sussman. The Magic of Walking. New York: Simon and Schuster, Inc., 1967.

Hittleman, Richard. Yoga: 28 Day Exercise Plan. New York: Bantam Books, 1981.

Johnson, Harry J., M. D., with Ralph Bass. Creative Walking for Physical Fitness. New York: Grosset and Dunlap, 1970.

Marchetti, Albert, M. D. Walking Book. New York: Stein and Day Publishers, 1980.

Epilogue

The journeys of the pilgrims and walkers of old and new times epitomize a universal and perennial need of human beings--the need to fulfill a meaningful life. How can one fulfill this yearning? And, more specifically, how can one find ultimate meaning? Great beings from all times--known and unknown--have been blazing trails to the Holy Land, the Temple, or the Rainbow of Meaning. But many of these trails are not accessible to all people, nor is the footwear that they require fit for all of us. Today we need a path of fulfillment which is possible for the common people: the workers in the assembly lines, the farmers in the fields, the wife or husband in the household, the drivers on the freeways, the students in the colleges.

There is an answer to these questions, and according to our experience it has two parts. The first is that every person can fulfill his or her human and divine possibilities by transforming daily life into a spiritual practice. Walking is an ingredient of daily life which provides a good starting point. By doing so, one can gradually perfect one's relationship with all the aspects of life. Walking keeps the body physically fit, the mind still and alert, and the soul joyful. Sightseeing and exploring while walking deepen our reverence for nature. The dialogues and sharing of communal hikes and family strolls create conviviality. The contemplative silence of the solitary walker opens one to the Eternal Presence. Thus, what we call Walking with Contemplation, others may call the Yoga of Walking, the Zen of Strolling, the Asceticism of Hiking, or the Tao of Sauntering.

Other ingredients of daily life are working in a job, driving on a freeway, cooking at home, studying in a college, and so on. Therefore, we could also begin or continue a path of fulfillment Working with Contemplation, Driving with Contemplation, Cooking with Contemplation, or Studying with Contemplation. In any case, the important thing is to do it in a conscious, continuous, and scrupulous way.

The second part of the answer is what we have verified in our walks by studying the lives of many great beings. Fulfillment of a meaningful life is giving of oneself. The specific ways that those great beings gave of themselves were different according to their personal characteristics and circumstances: the way of science, education, humanities, social action, religion, and so on. But there was something similar which gave fulfillment to their lives and today blazes the trail for us. They lived with a single intention, to fulfill their vocation, and their basic attitude was one of Participation.

Addendum

A Walker's Invocation

* * *

Blaze,
O Resplendent One,
The good path of my life.

* * *

An invocation helps a person to change his or her
state of mind from the habitual state of preoccupation, anxieties, or weariness toward a more expansive, alert, and joyful state. A good practice is to
learn the above invocation by heart and to repeat it
any time one begins a walk. This could be the daily
walk of a program for physical fitness, the walk from
home to the bus stop, the walk for reflection, or any
other kind of stroll, walk, or hike. One recites the
invocation with an intention of opening and uniting
oneself with life during the new day or time. Experience demonstrates that the practice of this or other
similar invocations produces surprising and beneficial
changes in the attitude of a person. What is required
is to practice it with attention, every day, and with a
proper tone and good intention. One must always
remember that the transformation of daily life into a
spiritual practice is based on the trinity of conscious-

ness (thus, attention), continuity (thus, every day), and scrupulousness (thus, proper tone and good intention).

Cafh Foundation sponsors a variety of activities for stimulating spiritual unfolding and has chapters in the following areas: New York, the San Francisco Bay Area, Los Angeles, Saint Louis, Washington, D.C., Boston and Chicago. For information write to
Cafh Foundation